The Survivor's Guide to Leaving

Sheila White
with Rachel Lloyd

Girls Educational & Mentoring Services

DEDICATED TO
Jasmine, Felicia, and Alicia
You will forever be in our hearts.

This guide wouldn't have been possible
without the amazing contributions, time and
dedication of our GEMS members and alumni.
Thank you for sharing your experiences and wisdom!

Cynthia	Dee Dee	Leslie	Melanie
Ericka	Yesenia	Courtney	Janira
Jennifer	Tamika	Yvonne	Kimana
Sondrah	Marisol	Mary	Aileen
Ashley	Paris	Shanay	Jordan
Angie	Kristina	Farah	Pamela
Nicole	Cassandra	Ivy	Jessie
Eliza	Abby	Naomi	Danielle
	Josalyn	Lakisha	

CONTENTS

Welcome

First, we want to let you know that, even though we haven't met you (yet!), we're proud of you—wherever you are in your journey. Whether you're taking the first steps to a brighter future or you've been out of the life for some time, as your sister survivors, we're here for you every step of the way.

Let's be real—

getting out of the life, leaving the game, healing from commercial sexual exploitation, recovering from being trafficked, however you want to say it, is HARD! We've been there, and we know how difficult, frustrating, scary and overwhelming it can be. Because we've been there, we also know that IT GETS BETTER! ☺

While all of our individual experiences might look different, we've found from talking to each other over the years that there are a lot of things we have in common. Knowing that someone else has been through it and made it out stronger has encouraged us, so now we want to encourage you.

We did our best to design this guide so that it doesn't stand out and look anything out of the ordinary. If you can't safely carry this guide around or may be worried that someone will find it, please consider leaving this guide at a friend's house who you trust, at a program, or a safe place where you can access it whenever you need to.

You might be wondering,

Will I ever feel normal?

How can I learn to trust anyone?

Why do I still miss my pimp sometimes?

Should I go back to school?

As survivors, we've asked these questions ourselves. As advocates, we've worked with hundreds of girls and young women who've asked these questions and more. We definitely don't claim to have all the answers! Sometimes the answers aren't even clear. But we wanted to share some of the things that have helped us get through, let you know that you're not alone, and that your feelings (whatever they are) are normal.

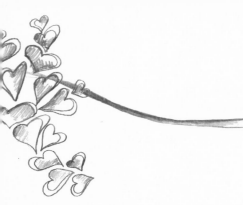

Love Me

Don't Judge Me

WE SUPPORT YOU!

You'll find inspiration amongst our voices, experiences and find the strength that's in you

We want this guide to support and empower you through whatever your experience may look like right now and wherever your journey leads you later on. You'll find questions, answers, stories, tips and ideas about how to make it through the recovery process. This guide is not intended to take the place of going to counseling, being in a treatment center or seeking outside support from a local agency or organization. We strongly encourage you to work individually with a counselor or someone you trust, create your own support networks, and establish therapeutic outlets to process the things you've been through. You may feel totally alone right now, but we know that there are people out there to support you in your journey.

We also want you to know that there's HOPE! ☺ We've all been in the life and made it out on the other side. Like anyone else, we still go through challenges in our lives, but we're so much happier, stronger, healthier and safer than when we were in the life.

Whether you are just leaving your pimp, contemplating going back, or have been out for a while but are still struggling with emotions or stigma, we hope you'll find inspiration from our voices and experiences. We know you can find the strength within yourself to keep going, just as we have all been able to do.

We
believe
in you

The journey is your own and we are here for you.

In this guide you will find these sections:

Understanding
What's Happened
To You

**Taking Steps
To Leave
The Life**

We've created these sections partly to make it easier to read 😊, but mostly because we recognize that recovery is a process with different stages, and there are different things we need at various points in our journey. There's no set timeframe for any of these 'stages', just as there's no magic moment when we move from one place or emotion to another. In fact, we often go back and forth between different points. Leaving the life and recovering from what we've been through is complicated and messy, but it can be helpful to understand which stage we might be in, in order to be patient with ourselves.

This guide was written by survivors of commercial sexual exploitation and trafficking at GEMS. Most of the contributions come from members, some from alumni who are now on staff, and some from our founder and other survivor staff. Because we're all GEMS folks, you'll notice GEMS mentioned throughout as a place of support, as somewhere we came to live or work, of a community that has meant a lot to us in our recovery. We don't want to make it seem like GEMS is this perfect place, or that GEMS is the only place to get support or services, but we know that in many locations there aren't programs like GEMS yet. In fact, that was one of the main reasons we were inspired to write this guide—so that we could connect our sisters across the country to other girls and young women who are facing the same challenges.

There are, however, a growing number of programs in different cities and states, and

ANYTIME YOU SEE THIS SYMBOL

IT MEANS THAT WE STRONGLY ENCOURAGE YOU TO TALK
WITH A COUNSELOR OR A SUPPORT PERSON
IF THINGS COME UP FOR YOU.

Starting Over

Adjusting To Something New

Continuing Your Journey

more and more people who are working on this issue. Some of these programs are survivor-led, some are survivor-informed, and some are run by allies. There are some great programs out there, so at the end of this guide we've listed national hotline numbers that can connect you to programs near you for support, as well as sites of online survivor networks and survivor-led programs.

One of the phrases you'll hear us use a lot is 'support person', because we strongly believe that everyone needs at least one supportive individual in their life who can walk alongside them through their recovery. We've all had someone in our lives who has helped us get to where we are today, and we're fortunate enough to now have a support network. In the beginning though, there was often just one person who we were able to trust and connect with, and we built other relationships from there. Sometimes our support person just appeared

in our lives. Sometimes we had to seek them out. You might find your support person through a program in your local community. It's awesome if your support person is also a survivor of the life, but it's ok if they're not. They can be a survivor of many other things, an ally, a counselor, an advocate, a social worker, a therapist, a guidance counselor or a mentor. In fact, their title is less important than the qualities they bring to the relationship. Even if you can't physically get to a program in your area, you can connect online with other survivors or call a hotline. Building a community of support especially with other survivors will be invaluable.

ANYTIME YOU SEE THIS SYMBOL

IT'S A TIP BOX.

What to Look for in a Support Person

* Authenticity (keeping it real)

* A sense of humor

* Good listener

* Empathy (not sympathy)

* Empowering not rescuing

* Honest – doesn't promise to make everything better

* Consistency – does what they say they're going to do

Don't Forget

Take time to relax and just breath. On pg. 52 are tips just for that!

I spoke to my mentor, and she suggested I go to a therapist. I was skeptical that this was going to work, because I been in foster care since I was 9 and a therapist is someone who had little to no effect on me and my life in the past. This therapist was a specialist in my trauma and PTSD. She was awesome, and I never thought that I would find a person like her to help me with my past and present problems with my life. I will always remember her, because she had not only listened, but she gave me what I was missing. She was a person I could share my most painful and my happiest moments. She had a great point of view, and never made me feel like I was stupid or emotional. One of the things she told me was to live my life with no regrets. I have overcome so much and nothing has stopped me, and she has helped me realize that I have so much to look forward to regardless of what I been through.

—Cynthia

This guide was written by girls and young women that were in the commercial sex industry. We have collectively shared our experiences to shape this guide so that it can be helpful to individuals who have gone through or currently facing similar experiences . Our hope is that other programs will also create supportive and empowering resources that give voice to the experiences not expressed in this guide.

We recognize that no two journeys are the same but we hope that **YOU** (no matter your experience, gender or sexual orientation) find this guide as helpful and supportive as we intend it to be.

Take your time with the guide. You don't have to read this guide cover-to-cover in one sitting. You can pick it up when you need it and read the parts that feel relevant to you at the time, or read it every day for encouragement. There's no right or wrong way to use it. We just hope it's helpful to you!

Understanding
What's Happened to You

13 and getting loved from the man I call my father,
I've tried to push him out of ME but why bother.
He's been raping me for as long as I can ponder,
 No dignity, no pride. SHIT, no soul left inside.
I have no more fight 'cos my body's tired

A man in a suit offers me LOVE and affection,
Too bad I was desperate and needed resurrection
He told me my body was made of gold.
That if I let guys do what my father did
 The money would unfold

Scared, confused, needed some guidance,
 Afraid to go home, because of the violence.
I accept this offer 'cos it seemed better than before,
No feelings, just numbness, no thinking no more.

Beaten for meeting this guy's satisfaction,
Afraid to go home because of my Dad's reaction
 I was made into an object for another's purpose only,
NOBODY ever asked me 'was I happy?,
       or 'why I was lonely?'

            -Dom

If you're reading this guide, you can probably relate to some or many of the things shared in the poem. While the specifics of your situation may look different, ultimately, we've all experienced trading sex. Most of us were children when we got into the life. Most of us had a pimp. All of us felt like, at one point, it was our only choice for survival. As young people, there are laws to protect us from adults who try to take advantage of our age and vulnerability, like statutory rape laws. These laws, however, haven't protected children or adults who are in the commercial sex industry, and have instead treated us as criminals who should've known better.

Even as adults we didn't choose to be in the life. There were a lot of things happening in our lives prior to being involved in the commercial sex industry and long before we became "legal" or legally able to consent to sex. We often tend to blame ourselves or think that our circumstances were different just because we were over the age of 18 or legally considered to be an adult but the same risk factors that played a role and made us vulnerable in the first place are the same regardless of what age you are. Survivors like you are fighting, and it's slowly beginning to change

Whether you got into the life at 12 or 20, whether you had a pimp or not, whether you were called a 'prostitute' and a whole bunch of other disrespectful names.
The feelings of shame and hurt are the same.

For the rest of this guide, you'll never see us use these words again. They are not true, they do not define our experiences, and, honestly, they hurt. Oftentimes, we've tried to take the sting out of these words by using them to describe ourselves and what has happened to us. We've heard them used so many times that we've begun to believe that's who we are. For this reason, it's important for us to truly understand what has happened to us, why we made some of the 'choices' we made, and how to accurately define our experiences.

While watching the documentary, Very Young Girls, I began to break down and cry because I didn't know what I was watching. I just saw that all the stories of the girls had been similar to mine. It was the first time I found out that I wasn't alone, and there were a lot of girls who had been through the same experiences as me. Never fully healing from such a tragic chapter in my life, I felt ashamed, embarrassed, and believed that everything that I had experienced in the game was my fault, and that I should of have known better because I was 18 at the time. Once I got to GEMS, I didn't know what to expect and was really skeptical about the program.

But the feelings I had felt once I participated in the groups and received counseling, I felt as though people genuinely cared, could relate and understand me. As time went on, I began to ~~xxxxxxxx~~ realize that it didn't matter what age I was when I got into the life because I didn't deserve what had happened to me. It wasn't about me ever making a choice; it was about me not having any options growing up.

— Ericka

So what is commercial sexual exploitation of children?

Commercial sexual exploitation of children (CSEC) and youth is when a child or young person under the age of 18 trades sex in exchange for something, like money, food, drugs or a place to stay, or the promise of those things. Sometimes this is called 'survival sex', but while it's true that it may have felt like our only option to survive, we don't believe that we should live in a world where young people (or anyone) has to have sex in order to eat or have somewhere to sleep.

It's commercial because it's treated as a business. We're treated as a product. We're marketed and sold. It's sexual because it can be actually having sex or sexual acts, dancing in a strip club, doing pornography, escorting, etc. It's exploitation because it's someone with more power (usually an adult with the money, the apartment, the drugs) taking advantage of someone with less power (a child, a teenager, someone homeless, someone in poverty).

What about trafficking?
Isn't that when people get brought from other countries?

Trafficking, or domestic sex trafficking of minors, is the same as CSEC except that there is someone else profiting from the exploitation. Basically, that means a pimp. A pimp is someone you may see as a boyfriend or partner, but may also be a family member or a friend. You don't have to travel to be trafficked, although often we are taken to different cities and states, and you don't have to be from another country. That's why it's called 'domestic' trafficking, because it happens in the United States to children and adults who live in the U.S. Some people are trafficked for labor (like working in a factory or being a maid), but this guide is about those of us who have been exploited or trafficked for sex.

Traffickers (pimps) use tactics to control you, like keeping your ID, threatening your family, isolating you, branding you with tattoos, and other kinds of mental abuse and physical violence. The same thing happens to girls and women (and boys, men and transpeople) from India, Thailand and Russia as it does to children, youth and adults from New York, Portland, Los Angeles and elsewhere in the U.S.

Why are all these terms important to me?

If you're going through any type of legal process as a victim, a witness or a defendant, it can be helpful to understand these definitions. More importantly, it's about us understanding that what happened to us happens to people all over the world. That it wasn't our fault. Anyone can experience trafficking and commercial sexual exploitation at any age, at any given time. We didn't just wake up one day and decide that we'd always wanted to be in the game. It happened because we thought it was our only way to survive or because someone manipulated us. It happened because we didn't have a place to live, were in foster care, didn't feel loved, didn't have any money, were being abused...the list goes on. There are so many other things that occurred in our lives that made us vulnerable in the first place. For most of us, the pain and trauma began way before we ever got in the life. When we feel ashamed or disgusted by what has happened, or feel like deep down this is who we are, it's hard to move on. Having a new language and understanding for our experiences helps us move forward and be truly free.

(In youth leadership class), I began to ~~understand~~ understand that I wasn't alone in my experience and how some of the things that happened to me were not my fault. My circumstances of where I came from in foster care, not having a good support system, and craving a family and love were all the things that made me really vulnerable to a pimp. I never chose to be in the life and while attending Youth Leadership I made the decision to become an activist against commercial sexual exploitation because I felt strongly about putting a stop to this. I don't want girls or anyone to go through half the stuff I been through. I have seen such impacts being made from not only my voice but the voice of so many who have overcome their past too.

— Cynthia

WHEN I FIRST HEARD 'COMMERCIAL SEXUAL EXPLOITATION',
I DIDN'T EVEN KNOW WHAT THAT WAS OR WHAT IT
MEANT, BUT ONCE I BEGAN TO HEAR IT MORE OFTEN
AND HAVE PEOPLE TELL ME THAT I WAS A VICTIM, I
FELT ENCOURAGED. TO LEARN MORE ABOUT IT. THE WAY
I UNDERSTAND CSEC IS WHEN A PERSON OR PEOPLE TAKE
ADVANTAGE OF YOU, WHETHER THAT IS EMOTIONALLY,
BY PROMISING YOU LOVE OR A FAMILY, OR IT CAN BE
FINANCIALLY, TOO, LIKE FOR FOOD, CLOTHES,
AND FOR A PLACE TO LIVE. AND YOU ARE BEING PUT
IN THE POSITION TO DO THINGS THAT ARE SEXUAL IN
EXCHANGE FOR THESE THINGS AND FOR THAT PERSON
TO BENEFIT FROM IT.

-DEE DEE

I feel like I made a choice to be in the game, but staff at my program are saying that it wasn't my choice. But then the judge said I did make a choice, and my mother keeps blaming me. I don't know what to believe...

We know it's really confusing. Often we feel like we made a choice because we are being criminalized for prostitution, or there are people around us who are constantly putting us down and shaming us for being in the life. Even the way that society views girls and women who are in the sex industry sends us a message that it's our own fault, and we chose it because there's something wrong with us. A lot of people are ignorant and misinformed about our experiences, and unfortunately, we can't control what people say or think about us. What's most important is how we view ourselves and our own experiences.

It's difficult to look back on our entry into the life and realize that we might have been manipulated and taken advantage of. None of us want to think of ourselves, or our situation, in that way. However, we also didn't think that being in the life would be amazing, or that we wanted to get hurt, trade sex, or experience any of the things we went through. We were vulnerable, whether it was our family background, growing up with abuse, being runaway or homeless, being desperate for shelter or money, or just being young and having adults around us who made us feel like if we did this they'd be there for us. We may have made certain decisions to run away, to get in someone's car, to go live with someone, to go work in a club, but that doesn't mean we chose to be victimized and hurt. Those decisions were based on a lack of other options at the time, or believing that this was the life we deserved. You don't have to figure out all the reasons behind those decisions. For now, it's enough that you know that you're not bad, dirty, or nasty and that this is all you're good at or good for.

It began from me taking a close look at my life growing up, and reevaluating the factors that played a huge part into why I got into the life. Identifying the things that were happening growing up that I had no control over allowed me to begin to understand that being in the life was not my choice. It wasn't my fault, and I wasn't the person to be blamed. My mother has her own issues of being sexually abused as a child, being physically abused by my father, and then struggling with an addiction, and she never dealt with her own issues. That's why she stayed on a path of denial and continued to take out her frustrations on me. My mother can't begin to understand why I entered the life, the level of abuse I went through, and all the traumatic situations I was in, because that is a constant reminder of all the ways she has failed me as a parent. She can't begin to process what I've been through if she hasn't processed what she has gone through and is still struggling with. She can't process how that affected me and how that led me into the life. It took me a long time to process and understand all of this. As an adult, I'm able to set strong boundaries now so that her issues don't impact my life. But as a child and a teenager, I didn't have any control over how her addiction and mental health issues impacted me and the 'choices' I made because of them.

-Selina

Over time, as you heal and recover from your experiences, you'll begin to figure out what choice really looked like for you, and why you were vulnerable in the first place. If that feels too confusing right now, don't worry, it'll come. What's important is that you know that you can move past these experiences. In this guide we'll be sharing experiences of how we've learned to make healthier choices that help us to protect ourselves. We know that you can't control everything; especially if you're underage, you can't make your own decisions about where to live, go to school, etc. We can, however, control our choices to stay away from certain people, to reach out to positive people, and to begin to be kind and loving to ourselves.

We deserve that.
You deserve that.

As often as you need to, even every day. Tape it to your mirror, or write it on a notecard and carry it around with you. You've heard negative things about yourself for too long, it's time to hear a different message.

WE BELIEVE THAT:

1. Commercial sexual exploitation and trafficking is something that happened TO ME - it is not who I am.

2. I'm not a criminal for being commercially sexually exploited and trafficked. I am a victim.

3. Acknowledging my victimization doesn't take away my strength and doesn't mean I will be a victim forever.

4. Although I may have made some choices based on my circumstances, I did not choose to be abused, violated, sold or treated as less than human.

5. I deserve to be treated with respect, and given services, love and support.

6. The real criminals are pimps and johns who buy and sell us, and they need to be held accountable.

7.   I deserve to live a life free of exploitation, danger, abuse and pain.

8.   I can heal and recover from my experiences, and go on to live a happy and healthy life. I am not forever 'damaged' or broken.

9.   I am not defined by my experiences or my past. I am more than what has happened to me.

10. I am beautiful, strong, unique and valuable. I have different talents and gifts inside of me, even if I don't see them yet.

11. I deserve to be loved, to have kindness, peace and happiness in my life.

12. I am a survivor.

Taking Steps To
Leave The Life

I keep feeling like I'm ready to leave but then I can't seem to go through with it.

Taking the first steps to leave can feel like a big hurdle to jump. The constant struggle between leaving and staying is something we've all experienced. Part of us wants to hold on to the familiarity of the life, the money (or at least the idea of the money), and the sense of love, attention and acceptance we received. The other part of us, believes that maybe there is something better for us. While we struggle back and forth between those two feelings, the daily shame, fear and guilt turn into numbness, and the idea of leaving begins to slip further and further away.

When you are stepping into the unknown, don't have any-where to go, no money to support yourself, and no one to really turn to for help, staying in the life feels like the only option you have. It's a difficult process that looks different for all of us. We all needed someone to help us through it, and we strongly encourage that you don't do this alone. If you are still in the life, reach out for support. No matter where you live, you can call the National Trafficking Resource Center's hotline number at 1 (888) 3737 888 or text BEFREE (233733) for additional resources. Both services are FREE and will connect you with someone in your area anytime, day or night. You can also look for local resources in the back of this guide.

Leaving the life, leaving him was one of the hardest things I've ever done. But as difficult as it was, it was the best thing I could have ever done for myself, because it was only then that I could finally live the life that I deserved all along.

—Yesenia

Even if you're not quite ready to leave, or have left and then gone back, try to find one person who you can stay in contact with who is not in the life and who you trust, whether that's a counselor at a program, a hotline worker, or a friend. When possible, it's good to have a plan, even if you aren't ready to carry it out yet.

1-888-373-7888

HEY ARE YOU UP?

HEY HUN ARE YOU OK?

NO NOT REALLY I THINK I AM READY TO LEAVE

OK. U REMEMBER WHAT WE TALKED ABOUT

It can feel like if you reach out for help or someone to talk to that you need to be ready to make changes immediately. Beginning the process of at least talking to a safe and trustworthy person doesn't mean you have to make a life-changing decision today or tomorrow. It's just the first step. We understand that there are often circumstances that can impact your ability to immediately get up and leave. Your well-being and safety are a priority, and we want to make sure that you are okay in whatever you decide to do.

What made it so hard for me was
the control, because when I did have folks he
made sure that I no longer existed. My Myspace was
deleted, my Facebook was deleted.

I had no friends.

NOBODY!

I didn't talk to my family, and so when I thought
about leaving, it was just really like, damn, where am
I going to go? And, does my family still want me?
It just made it really, really hard, and I had no plan.
In the beginning, when I first tried to leave, I went
back because I had no plan. So that made it hard,
because I just knew I wanted to get out, but when you
don't have a plan, you just set yourself up for failure,
and then you're going to go back to what's
easy and what you know.

Tamika

When I first tried to leave him I left for a few hours and went right back. It was hard. I loved him. He was my world. Watching TV didn't feel right if he wasn't there. Sometimes I just thought about leaving, and then I would talk myself out of it because leaving meant being without him. And that was something that I was not ready for at the time. When I finally did leave, I was just plain tired of him and being in the life. I was tired of having to sleep with different people. I was tired of having to deal with everything. With my last pimp, I was his only girl for the most part so everything was on me. With other pimps before him, it was easier to leave because I didn't miss them. It was harder to leave the life because the life was all I knew. I was good at making money. I missed pimps chasing and all the attention I would get on the track. It's like I was addicted to the game, the money and attention. When I finally did leave years later, I was tired and fed up and ready for a new adventure in life. Squares are not as lame as all of my ex folks would make them seem.

~Marisol

SHOULD I GO?
SHOULD I STAY? I JUST DON'T KNOW...

Memorize a couple of numbers that you can call if you need help. Don't just rely on saving numbers in your phone; you may not have your phone when you need to call someone.

If you save numbers of support people in your phone, give them a code name, so that if he goes through your phone, he doesn't get suspicious. Let your support person know what code name you have given them in case your pimp does call them.

If you're texting or using the internet to communicate with a support person, delete any messages so as to not leave a trail.

Make sure any support person in your life knows when not to contact you, or ways that they might unintentionally put you at risk.

If you're in immediate danger, don't call a friend - call 911 first. We know that you may not always trust the cops, but if your life is in danger or you're being hurt, they should be your first call.

Leave a copy of your ID or other personal documents with someone who you can depend on.

55-624-8932

Pay attention to your pimp's habits. When is he gone for long periods? When might be the safest time to leave?

Pay attention to details about your pimp - his real name, his date of birth, specific addresses he goes to, things about his family. Memorize as much as possible; these things could be important later on.

Think about what your most valuable items are, and what you could carry in a small bag. If you had to leave in a hurry, what would be the five things you would take?

Identify a safe place that you can access quickly, especially at night - somewhere public where you have access to a phone, but not somewhere he is likely to look for you. That way, if you need to call someone to come get you, you have somewhere safe to wait. This might be a coffee shop, fast food restaurant, or laundromat.

CAUTION!

We know that when you're planning to leave the urge to stash money is very strong. This can be incredibly dangerous. It's not worth risking your safety to stash money!

Some of us pretended that we were doing our laundry so that we could take a bag of clothes with us. Some of us wore extra sweaters or shirts under our clothes, and slowly brought these things into a program or friend's house, so that he didn't notice our stuff disappearing. Some of us had to leave every single thing behind, and leave just with the clothes on our backs. It is difficult to do this, but your safety isn't worth the risk. Clothes, a phone, anything material can be replaced; your life can't.

I'm scared he's gonna come find me, he has friends and connections EVERYWHERE.

Be careful, and put your safety first. You might need to call the police, get a restraining order, go to a shelter, or take other precautions to protect yourself or your family. All of these things are scary and stressful. We understand the fear. We know what pimps are capable of. But, we also know that pimps are really good at making us feel like they can find us no matter where we go, and that we'll never be able to escape. Honestly, this isn't true. It's part of the mind control they use.

WE ALL HAVE THAT FEELING THAT OUR PIMP IS WATCHING US 24/,7 AND THAT HE KNOWS EVERYTHING. IT'S ONE OF THE THINGS THAT HOLDS US. I REMEMBER THINKING THAT MY PIMP WAS THIS IMPORTANT PERSON WHO KNEW EVERYONE AND EVERYONE KNEW HIM. HE WOULD COME HOME AND TELL ME STORIES ABOUT HIS DAY, AND TALK ABOUT HOW HE HAD RUN-INS WITH PEOPLE AND THE POLICE. HE WAS EITHER BEATING SOMEONE UP FOR NOT UPHOLDING PIMP LAWS OR WHEN HE FELT PEOPLE WERE DISRESPECTFUL TO HIM. IT WASN'T UNTIL I WASN'T WITH HIM ANYMORE THAT I WAS WATCHING "THE SOPRANOS" SEASON AFTER SEASON THAT I STARTED REALIZING THAT HE HAD ACTUALLY BEEN TAKING THE STORYLINES FROM THE TV SHOW, AND MAKING ME BELIEVE THAT HE WAS LIVING THAT LIFE. I WAS WATCHING AN EPISODE

OF "THE SOPRANOS" WHERE THEY HAD TO KILL
SOMEONE WHO RATTED ON THEM AND EVERY DETAIL
WAS WHAT HE'D TOLD ME HAD HAPPENED TO HIM. I
WAS MORTIFIED AS I CONTINUED TO WATCH EPISODE
AFTER EPISODE, REALIZING THAT EVERYTHING HE'D BEEN
TELLING ME WAS A LIE! BY THE END OF WATCHING ALL THE
EPISODES, I JUST FELT LIKE HE WAS PRETTY PATHETIC
AND, ALTHOUGH I WAS NAIVE, I KNOW THAT HE'D BEEN
CREATING THIS FAKE WORLD TO KEEP ME IN TO ISOLATE ME
FROM THE REST OF THE WORLD. HE WAS A HABITUAL LIAR.
CAN YOU IMAGINE SITTING THERE WATCHING "THE SOPRANOS" WITH
THE WORDS RINGING IN MY EAR KNOWING THAT HE'D MADE THESE
STORIES UP SO HE COULD BIG HIMSELF UP TO ME, TO SCARE ME,
TO MAKE ME THINK HE WAS A HERO? I CAN LAUGH AT THIS NOW,
YEARS LATER, AND KNOW THAT HE WAS TOTALLY MANIPULATING
ME. HE PROBABLY REALLY DID NOTHING ALL DAY, AND JUST CAME
HOME AND TOLD ME HE WAS DOING ALL THESE INSANE THINGS!
I DON'T KNOW. I LAUGH NOW, BECAUSE AS I SAT IN FRONT OF
THE TELEVISION WATCHING THE EPISODES, I THOUGHT IT WAS A
COINCIDENCE, BUT NAMES AND PLACES WERE JUST THE SAME AND
IT WAS EVENT BY EVENT, AND I WAS COMING INTO REALITY.
I WAS SEEING HIM AND THE WHOLE SITUATION IN A DIFFERENT
WAY. IT WAS LIKE WAKING UP. I STARTED LOOKING AT OTHER
THINGS DIFFERENTLY.
꞊ PARIS ꞊

meet me on the corner

yea Im going to the store

all samantha tonight

41

We are not saying that you shouldn't be careful, but we don't want you to live in constant worry and paranoia either. No one's situation is exactly the same, so that is why creating a safety plan with someone is extremely important. You should share your specific fears with a counselor or person you trust, so that you can come up with strategies that will keep you safe.

Here are some questions you can think about and talk through:

- What areas does he frequent the most? Are there areas he avoids?
- Does he have a car? Memorize the license plate.
- Who are his closest associates? Family? Other pimps? What areas are they located in? Where do they hang out?
- Does he own a gun or any other weapons? Do you know where he keeps them?
- Where are some places you can immediately go to be safe?
- Where are your nearest police precinct, fire-station and hospital?
- Does he know where your family lives?

After leaving:

- What are the specific things right now that keep you from feeling safe? Is it a general feeling of being unsafe all the time?
- Who can you call and talk to when you feel unsafe?
- What areas can you avoid? For example, can you change schools?
- Can you get a restraining order?
- Is he on parole or probation? Can your support person contact his parole officer about your safety concerns?

Remember, it's normal to have a generalized sense of fear and anxiety after an experience like this; that's part of the trauma. It can feel like someone is always watching you, or you may think you see him even though you know it isn't him. Keep a balance of being both aware and understanding that it's a normal response to an abnormal situation. Over time, the fear will lessen. Talk through your feelings, and always tell someone if something doesn't feel right or something out of the ordinary happens.

After this happened to me I am aware of my surroundings in detail. I was told I exaggerate situations like if I see a slow moving car or a person is walking behind me or if a guy is looking at me a certain type of way but I see it like its better to be safe than sorry. Be strong, live your life, do positive things to keep your mind occupied, and just try to be happy and not miserable. At the end of the day it's not going to make anything better if you don't try; it's only going to make you feel worse so keep trying. It's hard to go through this and move on but try talking to a therapist or a close friend. If you don't have family like me or been through foster care; you can start a journal and put your thoughts on paper. Read it over and over and make changes that's what I do and it helps a lot.

—Angie

I just left my pimp a few days ago, and I'm so overwhelmed right now. Part of me feels free and excited about the future, and the other part of me feels like maybe I'm making a big mistake.

It's totally natural to feel like this. Again, it's a "normal reaction to an abnormal situation". What you went through wasn't normal. It's not normal to be bought and sold, beaten and exploited. BUT...your feelings and reactions to your experiences aren't abnormal. How you feel is how you feel. That doesn't mean you always have to act on your feelings, but you do need to accept your feelings and not feel guilty. You're also not alone, many survivors have experienced the same feelings and challenges, and they've made it through. So can you, even if it doesn't feel like that right now.

The first few days out of the life are challenging and a mix of emotions. You may just want to sleep because you are tired, or you may not be able to sleep because you can't stop worrying. You may feel depressed because you literally have nothing to do. You may feel anxious thinking about everything you have to do and accomplish. You may be checking your phone every few minutes. You may feel restless and trapped, like you just want to run but don't know where. You may be ready to go back to the life because at least you knew what to expect. Hang in there! It's important to remember the reasons you left—you were tired of the way you were being treated; you wanted something different for your life; you wanted something different for your child; you didn't want to get sold, hit, threatened, bought, controlled, or exploited ever again. Whatever the reasons were, keep reminding yourself that it will only be the same, and probably get worse, if you go back. But, if you stay out, it's going to get so much better in time!

I miss you

Change your number! If you call your cell phone company and tell them you're being harassed, they will change your number for free. Although we're often reluctant to change our numbers in the beginning as it can feel like we're totally losing contact, if your exploiter can still reach you (or other people from the life can), it's going to be hard to focus. He'll probably blow up your phone for the first few days, and the temptation to answer will be strong, even if you think you just want to curse him out! Once you start talking to him, he's going to say everything he can to get you to come back and, in those first few days/weeks, it's easy to believe what he says. Just give yourself a little space. It'll help you think clearly. Don't think about never speaking to him again, just make a plan to not call him today. And then tomorrow, make the same plan!

Changing your number means that he can't keep calling or texting you, and it means that you have a little control back in the situation. It can be strange to be able to make choices after being under someone's control for so long, but the more we take back that control, the easier it becomes.

Take it one day at a time. We know that sounds corny, but it works! Sometimes you can only take it one hour or one minute at a time, and that's ok too.

Sleep and eat as much as you need to. Talk to someone supportive who can help you process your feelings, like a counselor or a trusted friend, and if possible, another survivor.

Be patient with yourself and your feelings.

Try not to make any big decisions in the moment based on your emotions.

I was scared, nervous, not knowing,
and it's just being scared of the unknown.

The square life was like another planet to me so it was like how am I gonna
do this this is what I'm used to and overall it just a bunch of mixed emotio
I left more than once. I would leave and something would seem to pull m
back or it seemed like one step forward, four steps back and that
would lead me back to the thought of going back but every time
I went back, it would get worse, mentally and physically.

I was scared because I felt like there was no escape. My pimp knew
where my family lived, where my little brother went to school
and where all my close friends lived. Every time I ran away he would
know exactly where to find me. Not only that, he had my ID, my birth

♡ Kristina

46

certificate, my social security card. So if I did leave, I had nothing to work with to get my life back. It took me <u>5</u> attempts to finally leave the life but I leave the life but I went to shelter and they referred me to a program for girls who've been exploited. I have never felt safer and more secure. He can't hurt me anymore. And now I can live my life and be myself. Leaving the life for good was the hardest thing I've ever done in my life. But it's the best thing that ever happened to me. I got an order of protection on my pimp so now the law is protecting me from him and his friends and family. I'm not scared anymore. And now I have the strength and and wisdom to do bigger and better things. My pimp always used to tell me "if you knew better, you'd do better". I guess I'm smarter than he thought.

Don't be surprised if for the first few days you feel really happy and excited, and then really depressed; or if you feel angry, that you never want to see him again, and then start really missing him. When you're in the beginning stages of leaving, there are many emotions that you feel, sometimes all at once. Here are some common ones:

ANXIETY

FREE

TRAPPED

ANGRY

LONELINESS

HAPP

yes!!!

CONFUSED

OVERWHELMED

RELIEVED

HOPEFUL

SCARED

ASHAMED

HOPELESS

This list is not comprehensive. We are sure there are probably a lot more feelings that you may be experiencing, and they may be all over the place. That's okay. Talk to someone about how you're feeling. Sleep, eat, and take care of yourself as much as you can. Figuring out your feelings can wait. It can be a roller coaster, but you can get through it.

Breathing
&
Relaxing

BREATH, RELAX, AND LET THE STRESS GO

We all have moments when things get too much for us. Whether its drama with our family or someone stressing us at our program and we all have learned coping mechanisms to deal with stress. Unfortunately most of the ways we are used to (like fighting, getting drunk or high, running away, cutting, or even going back to familiar but unhealthy people) bring with them even more problems. What we've learned, and are still learning every day, is to try to use different coping mechanisms like breathing, grounding, and relaxation techniques.

We all know that a lot of this stuff is easier said than done but we have to try to find better ways to manage our feelings when we are feeling overwhelmed, angry, frustrated, and stressed out. When things come up for us sometimes it is easier for us to explode rather than take a moment to breath, calm down, and process what is going on inside of our bodies. This section will help you begin to center yourself so that you can find different ways to navigate your emotions when you are feeling stressed and keep you grounded while you're on your healing path. It might feel silly at first, deep breathing, counting, focusing on feeling your feet on the ground but once you start doing it, you'll actually begin to notice the difference!

Come to this part as often as you want and as many times as you need! Even if it's every day, practice makes perfect! The more you practice these strategies the easier it will be for you to relax and calm yourself down even in the most stressful situations.

Breathing & Relaxing

Obviously we all know how to breathe! But what we want to start doing is paying more attention to our breath... Learning how to breathe intentionally, and paying attention to how you feel is important in the healing process, and it helps with everyday stress too! Here are some tips on how to practice intentional breathing...

To start, you want to get ready to breathe and to actually think about breathing while you do it.

Breathe in through your nose and out through your mouth...

Breathe in deeply and breathe out slowly.

Take a deep breath in for 3 seconds and a deep breath out for 6 seconds.

Try this for a while—breathe in for 3 seconds and breathe out for 6 seconds.

Breathe in feelings of calm and peace;

Breathe out any negativity and stress. Close your eyes and keep breathing.

Feel your breath travel through your body. Experience warmth and calm, and imagine the tension release from your body.

Breathe in, and breathe out...

 Just Breathe In And Out

Breathing & Relaxing

It's really good to practice this for at least 5 minutes a day.
You can do it when you first wake up or right before you
go to bed. Once it becomes part of your morning or night
routine, try your breathing exercises for even longer, 10
minutes or more. This is your time. Allow yourself to just
be present. You deserve to have some quiet time, some time
just for yourself. Pay attention to your breath- feel it in your
body, and allow your body to relax and be free.

These slow, deep breathes are also good to do when you
find yourself in a stressful situation- if you're on a crowded
subway, and getting ready to take a test. You don't have to
close your eyes, but you can just try to forget about everything around you for a minute, and slowly breathe in
through your nose, and slowly breathe out through
your mouth. Just breathe in and breathe out
and allow yourself this time.

Learn To Comfort
Yourself

Grounding

You might have heard a counselor or someone talk about 'grounding'. Although it sounds like being stuck in the house and not allowed to go out, it's also a name for dealing with stress!

Grounding simply means settling yourself into a peaceful space mentally even when, or especially when, things are crazy around you or you're feeling really stressed or triggered. We've all had those moments when we feel really upset, our mind is racing, our heart is beating crazy fast and it can almost feel like we can't breathe because we're breathing in and out so quickly. Those moments can escalate really quickly to all kinds of negative places where we just get more and more upset or we end up getting in a fight, flipping out on someone, running away, or even hurting ourselves. So it's important for us to learn how to comfort ourselves and 'ground' ourselves when things get tough. The time to practice breathing exercises, grounding or relaxation isn't in one of those heated moments when you're feeling most stressed. Imagine being really angry and then having someone come in your face and tell you to breathe! You're not going to want to hear it. At all!! But if you're practicing a few minutes a day when things are less stressful it'll be so much easier when the pressure's on to remember these techniques.

Grounding

- **Do a few easy stretches**—roll your shoulders up to your ears, and then let them drop. Do this 3 times. Roll your hand around in your wrist a few times. Let the stress go out through your fingertips.

- **Clench your hands** into a really tight fist; hold in for a couple seconds and then release. Do this 3 or 4 times. Try it with your feet too—clench up your toes, then relax them. Try to feel your tension move out of your body.

- **Plant your feet on the ground.** Try to really feel your feet on the ground- on the earth. Feel your presence in the world. Press your feet down. Put your hands on your knees if you're sitting or by your side if you're standing. Allow yourself to be present. Practice a few deep breathes with this grounding exercise.

- **When you're near a sink**—run warm water in the sink and wash your hands. If you have a nice smelling soap, with essential oils (like lavender or almond oil) it's even better... Pay attention while you wash your hands- tell yourself you are washing away your stress for this moment. Smile to yourself.

- **Look in the mirror** and tell yourself positive things! You deserve positive affirmations. Allow yourself to hear these things. You are strong. And beautiful, and deserve to feel peace and love. Breathe in and breathe out.

- **Try to remember a beautiful scene;** a peaceful walk on the beach, a beautiful sky, a walk in the woods, or seeing a rainbow. Allow yourself some time to picture it. Picture the waves, and allow yourself to feel the beauty and to be stress-free.

- **Active sports and exercise** also help our bodies deal with stress and trauma. If you like to play sports find something you can do; ride a bike or a skateboard or jog a few days a week.

- **Some songs** have a way of taking the stress away too. If you like music—create a playlist to help you relax. Listen to it... And breathe...

Grounding

Sometimes, if stress is getting the best of you, it is also good to stop what you are doing and in the moment take a few breaths. It is important to know what it is right now that's stressing you out or making you feel anxious. Try to pay attention to yourself and what's going on for you inside of your body. Think about what it is that is making you upset in the moment and think deeply about the way in which you want to respond right now. Pull out a piece of paper and write down your feelings and reactions. Talk about these things with a counselor or your support person to help you process what is bothering you and how you can cope with your feelings.

Now think about the ways you deal with stress. We all have coping strategies. Some of them are really good for us, like counting to 5 or 10 before we react to something and some ways might not be so good for us, like smoking cigarettes. Think about the ways in which you cope right now. When you are stressed what are the things you do right away or in the moment? Are they good ways to deal with stress or not good? It takes time to figure out and see the healthy and unhealthy ways in which we cope with our stress so be patient with yourself. We encourage you to talk to your support person to come up with a list of both the healthy and unhealthy ways you cope so that you can create a strong support plan moving forward.

Sometimes when we are stressed out we tend to seek out other situations or people who aren't good for us just to take our mind off of what is going on. Whether that is meeting up with friends to hang out or calling up an ex to meet up. It can also feel much easier to go to a party rather than try to sit still, breath, relax and deal with our emotions. We often convince ourselves that if we don't think about it, whatever is bothering us will go away. Actually it doesn't go away and what we come to realize is that pent up frustrations, emotions, and stress can come out in A LOT of different ways.

Being aware of what stressed you out, writing it down, figuring out what you are feeling in the moment and why this thing, or person is so stressful or triggering to you is SUPER important. The more awareness you have, the better prepared you will be.

And sometimes, it is good to have someone to talk to. If you have someone who you know helps you feel calm and safe, call them. Talk to them, and get some calming vibes.

Remember—you can learn how to de-stress on your own. Allow yourself the time and space, close your eyes, and slowly breathe in through your nose, and breathe slowly out though your mouth.

Breathe in...
And breathe out...
Breathe in peace.
And breathe out the stress.
You are worth it.

It's HARD NOT KNOWING WHERE TO START FROM,
WHERE TO PICK UP THE PIECES. COS WHEN YOU LEAVE
YOU GOTTA LEAVE EVERYTHING BEHIND. SO, NOT KNOWING
WHERE TO START FINANCIALLY, IT'S A LOT OF CONFUSION.
SO, IT'S A LOT OF DIFFICULT THINGS YOU HAVE TO GO
THROUGH IN THAT FIRST STEP OF LEAVING

−CASSANDRA

Starting Over

I've done some things that I am <u>Not</u> proud of.
Not to stand out, or simply for attention
I've done what I had to do to survive.
At 16 years old, I have better survival skills than most

Knowledge is power
Experience is crucial
I've laid down morals
I've bargained for dignity
I've auctioned off my body
All in the name of survival

When I lay down at night, there is more to me than
that I am not just a survivor.

Resource finder

I am a conqueror
Strategizer
Goal achiever

At the end of the day I am a GEM

☺ Danielle

When we left it was winter time.
We had no clothes, no shoes....No nothing....
My daughter was in a onesie in the snow. I had to take my shirt off, I had a bra on, take my shirt off and wrap it around my daughter. She was 6 months. They did not want to help us. Even though we had scars and everything, they refused to help us, so I had to go through the whole process of begging people, and it hurt because I'm not used to asking people to help me.

-Natalie

Starting over is difficult,

but it is a huge step, and it's the first of many that we all had to take. Asking for help, especially when there have been people in your life who have let you down over and over again, is hard, but leaving without support is even harder. Even though you've been hurt and disappointed, we promise you that there are good people in the world who are coming from a good place, and who can actually help you. Trust is something that people will have to earn over time, so use your instincts and judgment, but give people a chance to support you.

Leaving was not easy for me, and I went back a few times. But eventually, I did it with the help and support of others. I looked for love in all the wrong places, as many people do, but that's life and we all make mistakes.

LOVE

The road looks hard and impossible. I never thought I would see past the life. It was hard for me to ask for help when I was so used to dealing with all of this alone, but there is help so DON'T be afraid to ask.

~ Lakisha

I was so scared when I left, and I felt like I my life was in danger even when I was with people who were trying to help me. I was brought to a place that understood me and what I had gone through. I felt like this place was made for me to start over and begin a new life. I began to work with a counselor who knew how to work with me and who understood about the life. She showed me how to get my life together. Getting my state ID, birth certificate and social security were things I felt I would never be able to get back after I lost everything. It took some time, but I accomplished it with the help of my counselor. My counselor knew I had a hard time reading and writing.

So she showed me what I needed to get, was there when I had trouble reading, and even helped me fill out the parts I didn't know. She took me to the offices that I needed to go to. Even though we went together, I still felt like I accomplished something because I would have not thought twice about it if I was in the life. This was a life changer for me, knowing I can do all these things for myself with the encouragement and support of my counselor. Some time passed, I started to get frustrated plenty of times, and I wanted to go back. I hung in there, and it eventually worked out for me. I will never forget the day I applied for housing and got it.

                                              −Abby

When we leave the life, we are normally leaving everything behind and starting over from scratch. Getting a new ID, birth certificate, Social Security card, clothes, toiletries, housing, Medicaid, are all things that require a lot of running around. Dealing with all those institutions and systems can be very frustrating. We know!! People are not always pleasant to us or helpful, and it's easy to feel like we want to give up or just curse out the lady at the welfare office! But, you can get through it. You just have to have a little patience (and in some situations, **A LOT** of patience!). Pace yourself, and take it day-by-day. Start with the things you feel aren't so hard first, like going to a homeless program that has clothing donations, getting a social security card, or getting your birth certificate. Then slowly work your way up to the harder things, like opening up a public assistance case, getting access to food-stamp benefits, or applying for long term housing. Sit down with your support person to prioritize your needs and come up with an action plan so you don't get overwhelmed. Although we want stuff to happen immediately, some of these things take time. See which things you can do on your own, and which things you will need someone to help you with. If your support person is a case manager or advocate, ask them what they can help you with, and a timeframe for when they can work on it. You have the right to hold them accountable, and they should be realistic and honest with you about what they can accomplish and when. Splitting up the tasks and working together means you can both stay on track and check things off your "to do" list as it gets done. Each time you check something off, you'll feel like you can conquer the next thing!

Not having any ID can be hard, but there were ways around that. I talked to my counselor and they were able to accept me into their housing program while working on getting my documents, like my social security card, state ID and so many other things that I needed. I thought getting everything all over again for like the hundredth time would be a headache, ~~but~~ but what I realize is that there are things that can be done to make that obstacle not as hard to go through, and I didn't have to go through it alone.

                                                        -Josalyn

Feeling trapped in many ways
caused me to fear my options
leaving me with no where to
turn. Even though the struggle
continues and it may seem like life
doesn't get any easier, the more I
go through in life the stronger
I become, and I can honestly
say that overcoming many
of my obstacles has given
me the strength to succeed.
Finding support groups and
surrounding myself with
positive people, created the
beginning to many pathways
for me. Being encouraged
and acknowledged for all
my hard work, motivated
and inspired me to do my
best always not just barely,
regardless of the many
obstacles in my way.

★ Leslie ★

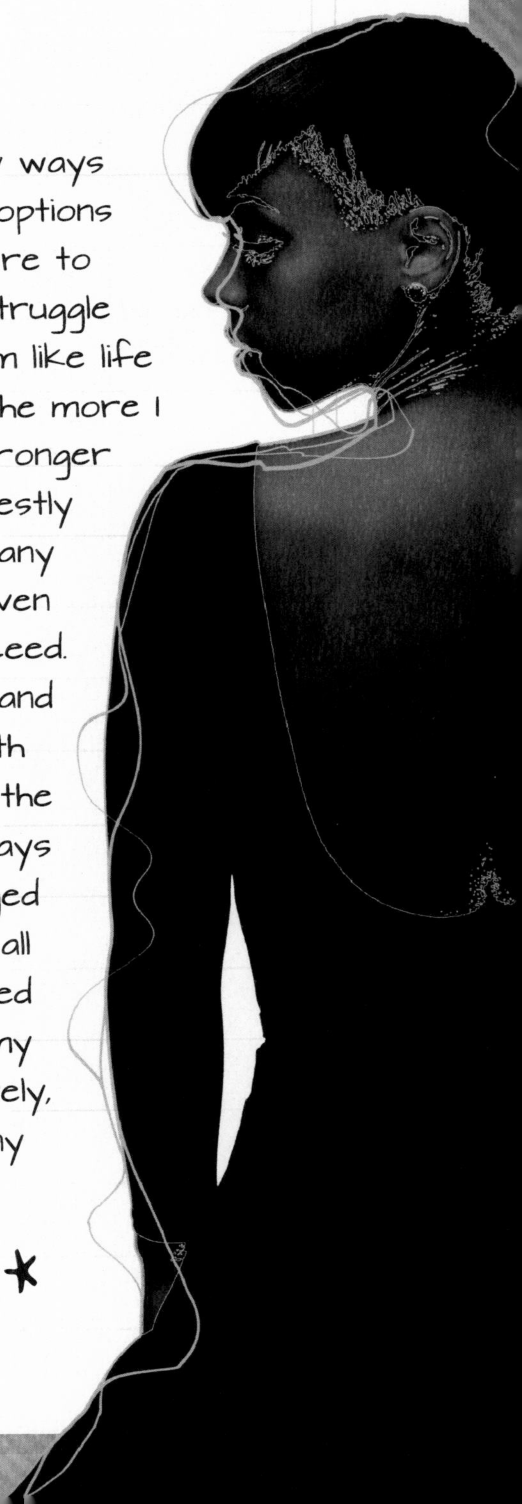

Yo I'm so tired of being broke now that I'm out of the life. I know it wasn't the BEST situation I was in but at least I had food, a roof over my head, nice clothes, a phone, and could get my nails done or go shopping. Now I've got nothing.

All of us have experienced the strain of being broke after leaving the life. It can be easy to look back and think we had it better before. But most of the time, we didn't get to keep the money we earned anyway, and even when we did, it was easy come, easy go. Regardless, we were in dangerous situations for whatever money we did make. When you're starting over and it's so tough financially, you can forget all the reasons you left in the first place, and it can be one of the main reasons you might go back.

Leaving the Life is difficult, like when you been in the Life for so long, and especially if that's all you know, and that's the only way you've known how to make your means. I'm 18 and I been in the Life since I was 14 years old. Four years, that's a long time one- and two, it's like how to transition from being this "bona fide hoe" to being square, and living Life regularly, and being broke, and my phone is off, and I don't have $52 dollars to pay my phone bill, and I can't go walk the strip? It's overwhelming, it's confusing, it hurts and, at the same time, it doesn't. You just gotta leave it behind. And that's the best way to just suck it up and keep it pushin.   –Yvonne

In the life, money doesn't seem to have any purpose or value because as quick as it comes is as fast as it is spent. It seems like there's always something to gain or work towards, especially when he's filling your head with the idea that you're 'building' together and towards your future. We also tend to spend money or get things in the life to help us feel better when we're sad or depressed, and in the moment, it gives us a high. Coming out of the life and not having money or a sense of what the future holds, is a really scary feeling. It can make us feel anxious on both a practical and emotional level. Even when we might be in a program where we have food, shelter and our basic needs met, not having money in our pocket can make us feel depressed. In the beginning there's no easy answer to this, but it doesn't stay that way forever. It's a process, and you have to give yourself time. Eventually, you will have a job, earn money that is yours to keep and that you didn't have to be exploited or abused to get. In the meantime, be resourceful, and remember you're still a valuable person whether you have money in your pocket, or not.

THE MOMENT THAT REALLY STUCK WITH ME WHEN I FIRST LEFT THE LIFE WAS WHEN THE PASTOR AT CHURCH SAID, 'IF YOU DIDN'T HAVE SUCH A BIG GAP IN YOUR HEART AND FELT BETTER ABOUT YOURSELF, YOU'D NEED LESS MONEY THAN YOU THINK YOU DO RIGHT NOW'. I FELT LIKE HE WAS TALKING DIRECTLY TO ME, AND THAT BECAUSE I FELT SO LOW ABOUT MYSELF AND HATED MYSELF, I TRIED TO COVER UP THOSE FEELINGS WITH MAKING AS MUCH MONEY AS POSSIBLE AND BUYING THINGS. HE WAS RIGHT. AS I STARTED TO HEAL AND LEARNED TO LOVE MYSELF, I NEEDED LESS 'THINGS' TO MAKE ME FEEL BETTER ON THE INSIDE.---DEE DEE

I had trouble finding a legit job with my criminal record, but eventually, I did. The key was, everyday I would try and at least put in one application somewhere. I eventually caught a break and got a job at a live music club. It was a job that I will forever be grateful for. From there, I just maintained and focused on having patience; everyday building on my future somehow, even the smallest efforts were significant.

-Eliza

The game is all I know and all I will ever be good at...

IT'S OK TO BE NERVOUS AND UNCERTAIN. TO BE HONEST, YOU ARE STILL GOING TO FACE MANY CHALLENGES AHEAD, AND IT'S OK NOT TO BE PERFECT. YOU ARE GOING TO MAKE MORE MISTAKES, AND THEY ARE GOING TO BE LEARNING EXPERIENCES FOR YOU IN THE FUTURE. IF IT INTERESTS YOU AND YOU THINK YOU MIGHT WANT TO DO IT ~~███████████~~.

GO FOR IT! THERE IS NOTHING THAT YOU CAN'T DO. IF YOU PUT YOUR MIND TO IT, THEN YOU CAN. THERE MIGHT, AND PROBABLY WILL BE, CHALLENGES ALONG THE WAY. AS LONG AS YOU KNOW THAT, THEN YOU CAN PREPARE YOURSELF AND FOR THEM.

~COURTNEY

When I made the decision to leave, it was something I really had to think about. My whole life was revolved around him at that point, my belongings, finances, and everything, down to eating and having a place to stay. I knew my family wouldn't help me because they already disowned me by that point. Spending most of my life in foster care before I met him, I dreaded starting all over again. Once I got into a program where other girls had similar experiences and were in leadership roles, I realized that starting over was just the beginning and it was possible. I was still young and I had a lot to look forward to.

— Cynthia

Even if you don't have a job right now,

eventually you will.

Even if you don't know what you're good at yet,

eventually you will.

In the meantime, ask a friend to help you brainstorm your skills, talents and things that you enjoy. Make a list of things that you do well, whether its being a good listener, putting together nice outfits, writing or singing. You might be able to utilize some of these things to help provide for yourself. Maybe you can babysit or do hair from time to time until you find a job. Maybe you can find a few programs that offer stipends for participating in events. Maybe you can sign up for focus groups where you get paid to give your opinion on new products. Maybe you can volunteer at an animal shelter or a nursing home, and start building a resume. Don't limit yourself! You'll discover that there are actually many things you are talented at and can excel in. When we find the things that we're good at and passionate about (and we all have those things), somehow the money and opportunities follow. There is a real sense of accomplishment and pride in doing something you love and doing it well.

You deserve so much
more than being in the life.
The game isn't the only thing
we will ever be good at!!

Having a job has changed my life completely. I will never forget the first time I cashed my work paycheck. When I watched the teller count out the money, my heart skipped a beat and I tried my best not to seem too excited! I recounted the money before I left the window, and once again as I tried to casually walk towards the door, but I felt like I was running. I couldn't wait to go shopping for myself, and do what I wanted with my money. Even though deep down I knew it wasn't all the money in the world, and I couldn't buy or get everything I wanted right at that moment, at least I had my own money and I could spend my check however I saw fit. All the money in the world couldn't amount to the happiness I felt, and I didn't have to give anyone anything or do anything I didn't want to do for it. It's been a big adjustment coming from a life where money had no sense of value, because at the end of the day money always mattered more than I did. But this is my starting point, I am invaluable and no amount of money could ever define what I am worth. I have a lot to offer, and I can actually do anything, including working a normal job, and looking down at my paycheck with my name, on it proved I could do it. Standing there, something washed over me. I was finally leaving everything I went through behind me, and this is how life was intended to be for me all along. I made it this far and I know now it is possible for me to keep going.

                                                    -Selina

There be some days where I go without money

You can achieve anything you put your mind to, and you can go on to have a perfectly normal, successful life. What we have been through doesn't have to be something that will define who we are, or put a hold on what we are capable of doing in the future. We are all smart, beautiful, intelligent, inspiring, talented and courageous women. We all have the ability to overcome whatever obstacles are standing in our way, and the inner strength to accomplish our goals.

m happy. As long as I'm happy, I'm alive and I'm healthy. That's all that matters. -Gail

Adjusting To
Something New

I just started living at this new program and it's nice and all, but I feel so weird. I don't know anyone, and I don't know if I can stick this out.

Being in a new environment can bring up many feelings. It can feel really great to be somewhere new, and at the same time, it can feel overwhelming and scary. We often think that no one will ever understand what we have been through, and that they will always judge us. It's true that some people might judge us, but not everyone will. There are other survivors out there who have been through the same things you have, who can relate and help you get over the feelings that may hold you back. We also have to give people a chance, even if they haven't shared the same experiences, because they can still be there for us and support us.

When I first came to GEMS, I had a barricade up around myself and was unwilling to let it down. I was very much afraid of how everyone would perceive me, so I walked around as though I was so much different from everyone there, when the truth was that I was very much like almost every girl there. We all looked different on the outside, but the truth was that many of us were dealing with the same issues on the inside. Being a member at GEMS allowed me to see that there were others that went through my struggles, which in a sense, was therapeutic for me. Looking around at the young women that shared some of the same struggles as me allowed me to see that I was not alone, and that I did not have to go looking for love and support from someone that would never be able to give it to me.

-Pamela

I just got sent to this program, and they're talking about how the life was bad, and my folks never loved me. But I know he did, and I loved him too.

Being told that your experiences were 'bad', or that the person you were with didn't love you, can make you shut down. No one should pass judgment on your experiences. You did your best to survive in spite of what were really difficult circumstances. It's not about the life being 'bad'. It's about the fact that you deserve to have a life that is peaceful and happy, and that you are worth so much more than being bought and sold. It's not about your pimp loving you or not. It's about the fact that there's a type of love that is unhealthy and dangerous, and that makes us feel bad about ourselves. Everyone deserves to have love that makes us feel safe, respected and cared for, and where the other person wants the best for us. Most of us didn't get that type of love growing up, so we don't really know what it feels like. This love doesn't just come from a boyfriend or a girlfriend. It can come from different people in our lives who don't make us feel like we have to do something for them in order to gain it, and who don't put us in danger or hurt us—ever. In our experiences, as we began to meet people who were genuine and who gave us that type of love, it made us not want the unhealthy type anymore. It doesn't mean our feelings went away for our ex overnight, and it doesn't mean that we will necessarily hate that person today. It does mean that we began to see that being hit, being told/asked/persuaded/forced to have sex for money, being controlled, being made to feel worthless at times, or having to give someone our money, was not what we wanted in our lives anymore. Slowly, day-by-day, we began to believe that we are important, lovable and valuable enough to deserve so much better.

love: a feeling of strong or constant affection for a person

The second time I left, I went to DV housing, and I went to a group where they were talking about how the abuser says things, and then say they didn't say those things with ~~the purpose of~~ the purpose of making you feel like you are the one going crazy. At the time, I didn't really think about it, but I went back and he got in to it with one of the other girls and he was like F*** all of you. A few minutes later, we were talking about what he said. I told him about what he said and he told me he didn't say that, but I was right there when he said it and I know I heard him say it. It was then that I kind of had a light-bulb-over-my-head moment. I definitely knew I was over him, not just because of this incident, but because it was then that I began seeing him for what he was, a true abuser. I am happier now than I ever was with him. Now that I think back, I wish I knew how good my life was going to be, and how happy I was going to be. I would have left a long time ago. I'm saying it took me some time to get where I am today, and some days I did not think I was going to make it, but I'm happy I kept going.

Ü

Nicole

When I was in the life, I felt like he really loved me and that I was doing everything so that we could have a future together. Now that I'm out, and I'm looking back thinking about all the s*** he did to me. How could I have let myself get played like that? I feel so stupid.

You didn't do anything wrong to deserve what happened to you, and you are definitely not stupid. You have nothing to be ashamed or embarrassed about. Being in the life was not something you had control over. It was not something you chose to do. Your feelings and emotions are real, and someone shouldn't use, lie, manipulate or take advantage of them. We may not have always made great decisions, but we often made those decisions in the context of growing up with abuse, homelessness, or just being young. We are often our own worst critic and will blame ourselves for what happened. Releasing and 'forgiving' ourselves for those decisions will help us to heal. Otherwise, our own shame and guilt will keep us trapped even after we're physically 'free'.

happy!!!

yes!!

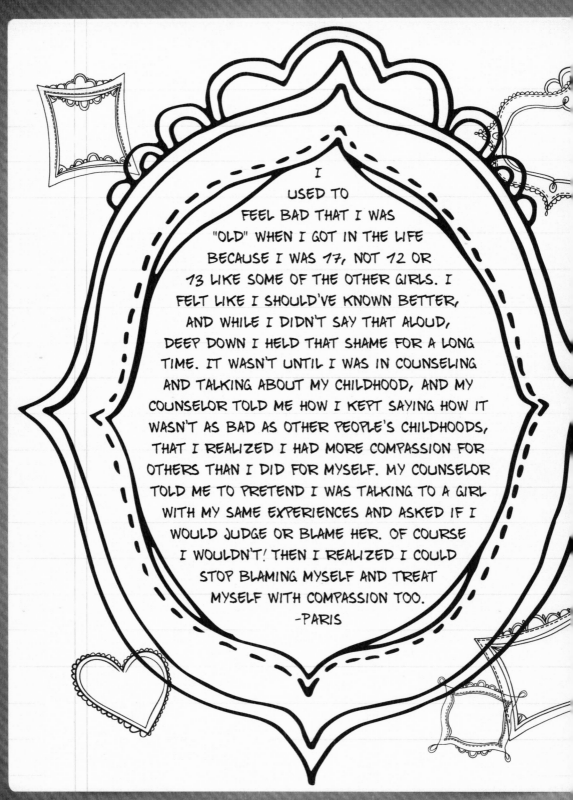

I USED TO FEEL BAD THAT I WAS "OLD" WHEN I GOT IN THE LIFE BECAUSE I WAS 17, NOT 12 OR 13 LIKE SOME OF THE OTHER GIRLS. I FELT LIKE I SHOULD'VE KNOWN BETTER, AND WHILE I DIDN'T SAY THAT ALOUD, DEEP DOWN I HELD THAT SHAME FOR A LONG TIME. IT WASN'T UNTIL I WAS IN COUNSELING AND TALKING ABOUT MY CHILDHOOD, AND MY COUNSELOR TOLD ME HOW I KEPT SAYING HOW IT WASN'T AS BAD AS OTHER PEOPLE'S CHILDHOODS, THAT I REALIZED I HAD MORE COMPASSION FOR OTHERS THAN I DID FOR MYSELF. MY COUNSELOR TOLD ME TO PRETEND I WAS TALKING TO A GIRL WITH MY SAME EXPERIENCES AND ASKED IF I WOULD JUDGE OR BLAME HER. OF COURSE I WOULDN'T! THEN I REALIZED I COULD STOP BLAMING MYSELF AND TREAT MYSELF WITH COMPASSION TOO.

-PARIS

Now that I have left the game, the "square life" feels so different and weird. Am I buggin'? Am I the only one experiencing this?

Nope, we all felt like that in the beginning. It's a big transition to make. It's hard not to feel like a square peg in a round hole. We worry about saying the wrong thing at the wrong time. We worry that we're going to 'give ourselves away' by doing something that square people don't do. What was okay and normal in the life is now the opposite in the square world, and we wonder if we're ever gonna fit in. Change is hard for every-one. Being in the life, we got used to the everyday routine. We knew the rules of the game. We had people making decisions for us. The square world works differently, and we can feel really lost having to make our own schedules and choices. Don't be embarrassed if you feel like you have a lot to learn or relearn. We've all been there. Find other people who can sup-port and guide you through the process. You're smart. It might take a little time in the beginning to adjust, but once you start figuring stuff out, there'll be no stopping you!

I struggled with figuring out how the square society functioned, feeling desperate for someone to just explain the rules to me, and feeling like I was doing something wrong all the time, always outta pocket, because I still had this loyalty to the game and loved him. Being around other survivors was so important for me to begin to feel normal again. Knowing that other people had the same experiences and struggled with the same feelings helped me so much.
      —Eliza

I've been out of the life a little while, but I'm so bored and depressed now.

The life is fast-paced. There's always some drama going on, and although it's mostly negative, we can miss that adrenaline rush. A lot of us also grew up in drama-filled homes, so when things get quiet or boring, it makes us nervous or depressed. We may even try to create drama just to 'feel' something again, because that's what we're used to. It takes a while to be okay with things being slow or kind of boring, especially if you're not in school, working, or surrounded by new friends yet. You'll have a lot of time on your hands to sit, think and get depressed. Over time, you'll find new forms of excitement that are positive, and you can begin to actually enjoy **peace and quiet in your life**!

Before everything, I was pretty quiet and I never went out much. Then I got into partying and doing stupid things for fun, just to be a part of the group. I would let people do anything to me, or convince me to do anything as long as drugs or alcohol was involved. I would do anything to be accepted. Now I don't party at all or do drugs or alcohol, because it reminds me of that time, and then I will be doing those things again. So now I'm back to being quiet and sticking to myself, but I still enjoy exploring new places wherever I go. I don't need to be accepted by everyone to have a good time.

♡ Jessie

I find that being around people that want the same things out of life that you want is what makes getting to a better place so much easier. It took me some time to find out what fun was, what makes me happy, and I sometimes struggle with that, but I feel like in time every thing will come.

-Nicole

I feel soooooo alone.

Everyone hates feeling lonely; it's not just us. But it can be harder coming from a life where you are constantly around people, constantly coming or going. You might miss the companionship of your wife-in-law, the intimacy and love you felt with your folks, or even the attention from being in the club or on the track. Feeling alone doesn't always have to do with having someone physically present. You can feel alone emotionally or alone in your thoughts. You can feel like you don't have anyone to talk to who would understand. There's not a lot of alone time in the life, but the truth is, we often felt very lonely. Now though, it's important to remember you are not alone. There ARE people out there who understand and can support you. Sometimes you will be physically alone when no one's around or no one's answering their phone. Learning to be okay with this takes time. Understand that to be alone doesn't necessarily mean you have to be lonely. It can be easy to latch onto the first person who'll pay attention to you or is just present, but be careful who you choose to be around when you're lonely. Often we end up choosing people who don't have our best interests at heart.

After I left my abuser, I was 16, I was less scared of him finding me than if he did find me what would happen? What would he do to me? I felt alone with no one to express my feelings to. I missed him, loved him and felt like I needed him. —Kimana

Create a strong support network. Write a list of 5 positive people who you can call to support you.

Join an online survivor support group. There's a list of survivor Facebook groups in the resource section.

I used to really struggle with feeling lonely. Sometimes I still do, but I try to just accept the times when I'm feeling like that and know that it will pass. Building good relationships with people, enjoying my alone time, and finding things that I like to do, and being peaceful with myself has changed my feelings of loneliness and the ways I used to try to fill it, like drinking or getting high or jumping into relationships just to have someone laying next to me. I've learned that I can feel more alone next to the wrong person than I feel laying by myself. Now, I make choices about who is in my life based on who can make me happier than I can make myself, rather than who can fill the gap I might be feeling.

– Abby

I really want to run away right now!!

We've all had that feeling, and many times we've acted on those feelings, but running away is not the answer. Even if we need to get away from an abusive situation, it's better to do it with support than end up alone on the streets again.

CALL THE NATIONAL RUNAWAY SWITCHBOARD 1800-RUNAWAY

THERE'S SOMEONE TO TALK TO 24 7, IT'S FREE AND THEY'LL LISTEN TO YOU AND MIGHT EVEN BE ABLE TO OFFER SOME IDEAS.

Sometimes you need to run away from things or situations when they are not good, but then if you get used to running, then you will run away from all the good things, too. When I can find one good person to keep me focused with a reason to keep going and believing in myself, then I will not keep running away.
Jordan

Running away can become a habit when you feel overwhelmed, or in a space where you don't know what is ahead of you. A lot of us have run away in the past, but being out there alone can make us vulnerable again. We can put ourselves in a dangerous situation or end up in a place where we don't want to be. Where you're at right now might really suck, but you won't be there forever. As long as it's not dangerous or abusive, try your best to stick it out and take it one day at a time. In those moments when you feel like running away, take a minute and think about what it is that is bothering you, then talk to someone about how you're feeling before you make a rash decision. Give people the chance to help. Allow yourself the time and space to work through your feelings, and things will begin to get better little by little, but you have to stick around in order for that to happen. Think of the place you want to run away from, whether it's a group home, placement or with family, as just a stepping stone to a place where you really want to be.

When I wanted to run away from my parents, I thought about all the negative things instead of the positive things. When I took a second thought on feeling like nobody in my family loves me, it kept me with so much negativity. As I cooled my mind with music that began to give me happy thoughts. I tended to change my moment of feeling depressed and what makes me change my mind of running away from all the people that wrong me is to get myself lost in my lovely imagination. To avoid many conflicts with many of my family, I sing in my head and tell myself I'm going to make it out in a positive way. Don't let anybody tell you that you are not going to make it. Keep in mind that you have a whole life in front of you.

Smile! -Janira

**I can't stop thinking about him!
I know he's no good for me, but I still
really miss him. Is there something
wrong with me?**

When I left the life, the first few
months I didn't have time to think
about being alone. I was running
around trying to get everything
together. That's all I was thinking
about, and getting some sleep. But
when all the running around was
done it was just me and time. I
started to think about him, and I
started to tell myself that we'd
had some good times and that
he wasn't all that bad.
Maybe we could work
it out. Maybe I should
just call him to say,
'hey' and to see if he
missed me.
            —Melanie

TIC

TICK
TOC

TIC

TICK
TOCK
TICK
TOCK!
TICK
TICK
TOCK!
TOCK
TOCK
TICKTOCK!
TICK
TOCK
TOCK
TICK
TICK

We know you are feeling alone right now. You can't seem to focus on anything in particular, or your mind is constantly wandering back to what he is doing without you and if he is thinking about you just as much. It may feel like your whole world is crashing down around you, and you feel so helpless and lost without him. It is hard to deal with the anxiety, fear and mixed emotions of wanting to be done, and still feeling stuck because you love him. Some people might not understand how we can miss someone who abused us in so many ways, but it's not that we miss being sold or being hit, we miss what we're familiar with. We often remember the good moments more than we remember all the bad ones. We spent a lot of time in the life suppressing how bad things really were, so it can take some time to realize that we really didn't deserve to be treated like that, to realize that the good moments here and there didn't outweigh all the pain we had to go through. Even if you still love him, try to hold on to the thought that love shouldn't hurt so much. It's ok to miss him as long as you don't act on these feelings. It's not helpful in times like this to call him, meet up with people who are still in the life, check his Facebook page, or start thinking about all the good times. Stay strong! These are feelings that will pass in time, and as long as you get through today, tomorrow you might see things differently and feel a little better. And, if you don't, there's another tomorrow after that!

When you start thinking about going back, or if you are missing him, write down how you feel. We strongly encourage you to work with a counselor or support person to process things that come up for you, and talk about the things that can be most helpful in moving forward.

It was hard to leave my pimp, in my mind, this was love, affection, and security. This was all I knew. So I stayed, and every time I thought about leaving, it was just a thought. I was not sure I would make it that far before he would find me. I even thought about choosing a different pimp because maybe this would make it easier. But my feelings for him kept me there. I ~~really~~ loved him, and I assumed deep down inside, he loved me too. I thought if I stick it out, one day it would be just me and him, until I realized different. After getting locked up numerous of times, raped and abused by tricks, I wondered was he REALLY protecting me. I started to question the love he was giving me, and I ask myself was this love worth dying for? No matter what the square life may bring my way, I wanted change, from getting locked up, from the abuse, and from all the false promises of a better life. I just knew if I can survive all of that, I can survive leaving him too.

–Lakisha

He kept calling my phone, and I kept picking up. He called me all types of bitches and hos. I cried, and I wasn't eating because he had me so stressed. My friend's mom pulled me to the side told me that if that man cared about me he wouldn't sell me and beat me. So I stopped answering the phone. I went to the store the next day and changed my number. I haven't spoken to him since.

                                        -Naomi

My Heart is Broken CAN you HeAr it?

When I was with my pimp, and even for a long time after I'd first left, I thought I would never love anyone like that again and that I'd never get over him. I thought about him all the time, and I felt like I'd never be truly free. Years later, he got in touch with me and it was so weird to see how all those feelings were totally gone. If anything, I felt a little sorry for him cos his life was so pathetic and he was in bad shape. And then I figured he deserved it for everything he'd done to me! It was hard to believe that this was the man who had controlled my life for so long and who had me under his spell. He tried to spit some game at me, and it was kinda funny to me that he really thought that the same lines that worked on me when I was a kid would work now I was grown and my life was so much better. You couldn't pay me a billion dollars to go back to him or go back to the life. Things aren't always perfect, but I'm so grateful that I'm not trapped in that world anymore, and that my life has turned out so blessed.

—Rayne

NO STRESS ZONE

Dear Stress,
Let's break up.
love, Me

Is it possible to love someone who doesn't love you? I know exactly what it feels like to love someone who simply doesn't love you. You see, he said he loved me, but he really loved what I did for him. When I left him at first it was awesome, but as time moved on, I began to miss him very much. I would even call him to talk.

But every time I missed him, every time I thought of going back, and after a few phone conversations I realized something; he would never change. The only thing that saved me was finding out that I loved myself more and understanding how to love myself. I haven't been with my ex folks for almost 6 years now.

-Jennifer

I stay stressed out.
Everything stresses me out.
It's just too much sometimes.

It's really important to figure out the things that make you feel better or calm you down. Even with a strong support system, there'll be times when no one's around to talk. In those moments, you have to find a healthy way to de-stress. We're often used to coping strategies that actually harm us more than help us, like having a drink or a smoke to chill out, having sex with someone who doesn't treat us well, spending money, or going to hang out in areas or with people who aren't the best influences. These strategies may relieve stress in the short-term, but can have a negative impact on us over the long-term.

Getting out the life was hard; I had to face many challenges. I found myself doing things to keep me focused. Think about it, if you're surrounded by negative people, you are not going to be focused, and those people don't care about you or your future. They're miserable, and as the saying goes, 'misery loves company'. If they're messed up and going down the wrong path, they will only bring you down with them. I say, do the right thing and don't give in to the negativity. Stay strong. As women, we are very strong creatures, and we have many gifts. Don't let nobody or nothing dictate your life.

-Iris

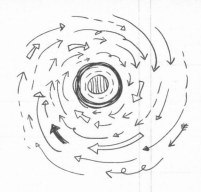

Things We Can Do to Make Ourselves Feel Better

1. Write in a journal
2. Pray
3. Listen to music
4. Go for a walk
5. Take a hot bath
6. Draw, paint, or make a collage
7. Take a nap
8. Watch your favorite TV show or a movie
9. Play cards
10. Read an interesting book or magazine
11. Exercise or dance in front of the mirror!
12. Create boards on Pinterest or create fashion looks on Polyvore
13. Play Candy Crush

ONE OF MY FAVORITE THINGS TO DO IS TAKING LONG WALKS IN THE PARK AND CLEARING MY MIND. TELLING MYSELF OVER AND OVER, IT'S GOING TO GET BETTER, STAYING POSITIVE, STAYING AWAY FROM NEGATIVITY, AND STAYING AWAY FROM NEGATIVE PEOPLE.

-SONDRAH

prayer

One of the most important things that's helped me the most is the Serenity prayer. I used to hear it all the time and I never really paid attention to it like that. But now I understand how true it really is.

A lot of what I've worried about or tried to control is the stuff that I really don't have control over,, especially how other people act. Realizing that I can only be responsible for how I react to stuff or what I do has been important and has helped me A LOT.

God, grant me the serenity to accept the things I cannot change, the courage to change the things I can and the wisdom to know the difference.

— Tamika

My program keeps saying that I would feel better if I went to talk to a counselor. But I don't trust therapists and counselors and stuff. I had to see a bunch when I was little, and they didn't help at all. How are they even gonna be able to understand what I've been through?

At first you may not want to talk to anyone about how you are feeling and what you are going through. A lot of us have had negative experiences with counselors in the past. We know it is extremely hard to trust people, especially people who we think won't understand what we went through, but finding a counselor or therapist to talk to is crucial. Having a space to vent when you are feeling overwhelmed by emotions and don't know how to deal with them, and having someone physically there to listen goes a long way. Not everyone is going to be the right fit, but it's worth trying. It has taken us some time to begin to trust, but what we have realized is that there are people who genuinely care, and are coming from a sincere and loving place. Not everyone is out there to hurt us, mistreat us, judge us, or make us feel like we're less than human. There are people who will help, encourage, motivate, and support us, wherever we are at in our healing process.

It was so hard, but I was like, 'You know what? I have to do what I have to do.' During this process I can say I met a few really good people. Complete strangers treat me better than my own family so I'm grateful for that. So, if it wasn't for complete strangers, God knows how jacked up we would be now.

—Casandra

It's hard for me to trust people, and if it's that first time, no matter what you say to me, I'm not going to be able to open up. But like if I'm consistently seeing you, like when I had mandated sessions with my therapist and I was always seeing her every week, after a while I built that trust, and I was like, alright maybe I can open up a little bit. –Aileen

Remember the counselor is there to serve YOU. If you don't feel comfortable, then you don't have to share. Ask the person questions when you first meet them. It's like interviewing someone for a job, a really important job of talking and listening to you.

Here are some suggested questions you could ask your counselor to get to know them better:

1. What led you to working here?
2. What do you enjoy most about working here?
3. What do you feel are your strengths when working with girls who have been in the life?
4. What do you know about the life and being in the life?
5. Have you worked with many issues of abuse before?
6. Why do you want to help me?
7. What can you do to support me when I want to go back to the life?
8. If I am going through something or need to talk, can I call you?

Don't feel like you need to share everything in your first few meetings. Choose what you want to talk about. Write stuff down before your appointment, if you like, and use it to guide the conversation.

Trust your gut instincts; if you really don't feel comfortable with someone, that's ok. There's someone else out there. If you feel like the counselor is pushing you to talk about something you're not ready to, tell them.

Plan some self-care for after your appointments because counseling can kick up a lot of difficult memories and emotions. It's important to have people to talk to afterwards or somewhere safe to go. Falling back on old coping strategies (drinking, smoking, etc.), will help calm you in the moment, but really doesn't help in the long run. It's hard to acknowledge our feelings, but that's kind of the point!

Remember, even though many people we meet may not have been in the life or share the same experiences, it doesn't mean they can't help or support us. We call those people "allies" because they're on our side. It also helps to remember that, while they may not be survivors of trafficking and the life, most people are survivors of something. We can't tell by looking at someone what they've been through, so we've learned not to make assumptions or judge people when they want to support us.

Every guy I come into contact with reminds me of a john. I feel like every man is a trick and it's bugging me out.

When you're coming out of the life your perception can be a bit blurry. Every guy you come across or interact with will most likely resemble or feel like a trick. You may think that all men just want to date you for money or only look at you or act in a way that is sexual. You may feel very uncomfortable around men because it's a constant reminder of what you've been through and how nasty and dirty you felt at that time. Or you may feel more comfortable around men than women because you feel like you know exactly what men want and you don't expect them to treat you well. We feel these things because we haven't experienced anything other than being in the life. We've been taken advantage of and used by men. We've been treated and seen as nothing more than sexual objects, so it's normal to feel like that's what every man wants and that all men are the same. Eventually these feelings will fade, but it's ok to protect yourself. Trust has to be earned, and not everyone should be trusted, regardless of gender. Trusting men can be especially tough.

There are good men out there. It's true! Over time, we've developed relationships with men as friends, as allies, and sometimes as fellow survivors. For those of us who are interested in men as partners, we have found healthy intimate relationships with them. In the beginning though, our trust and perception meters may be off, and you may find that you either trust way too easily or don't trust anyone. Finding a balance takes practice and healing.

My life

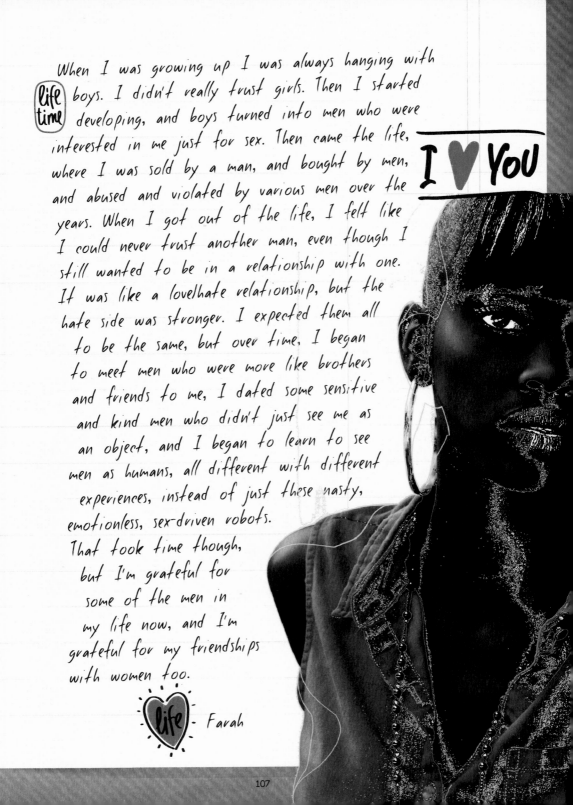

When I was growing up I was always hanging with boys. I didn't really trust girls. Then I started developing, and boys turned into men who were interested in me just for sex. Then came the life, where I was sold by a man, and bought by men, and abused and violated by various men over the years. When I got out of the life, I felt like I could never trust another man, even though I still wanted to be in a relationship with one. It was like a love/hate relationship, but the hate side was stronger. I expected them all to be the same, but over time, I began to meet men who were more like brothers and friends to me, I dated some sensitive and kind men who didn't just see me as an object, and I began to learn to see men as humans, all different with different experiences, instead of just these nasty, emotionless, sex-driven robots. That took time though, but I'm grateful for some of the men in my life now, and I'm grateful for my friendships with women too.

Farah

I ♥ YOU

I feel like I have a sign on my forehead, and that everyone can just look at me and tell what I've been through.

We automatically assume that people can look at us and just tell that we were in the life, but that is not true at all. There's no scarlet letter or a flashing neon sign on our foreheads. There is nothing different about us. We may have visible tattoos from the life, but that's something you can get help with covering up or removing. Even without a tattoo, we often feel that everyone 'knows'. We're scared around square people, thinking that at any moment they might find out and we'll be humiliated. We can feel like a fraud or a phony trying to live a square life, and that everyone's looking at and judging us. Generally, these feelings are our own judgment of ourselves.

I remember a couple of years after I was out of the life getting groped on the subway. I was so shocked; I just stood still and let it happen. I was so ashamed, and I felt like it was because the guy knew I'd been in the life, that I was nasty and all those other things. I couldn't stop crying afterwards. Then, when I started talking to other women who weren't survivors of the life, I found out that almost everyone had a New York City subway pervert experience, and it wasn't just me! It had nothing to do with me being in the life, and it was just my own shame that I still hadn't dealt with that made me feel like I was an easy target or the type of girl who was 'asking for it.

—Yesenia

We've talked a lot in this guide about letting go of our own shame, because we know it's one of the most important things in our journey forward. We can't change other people's opinions, and although the world is starting to change in how it sees this issue, there are still a lot of judgmental people out there. The harsh stigma that society places on individuals who've been in the commercial sex industry can push us back towards the life. At least there we'd feel that we wouldn't stick out; we'd be like every other girl on the track. But, while we may not have been judged in the life, we were violated, exploited and abused.

All kinds of people have survived things in this world that we would never know just by looking at them. Nobody can look at us and magically 'see' what we've been through. Even if they could, the truth is that they'd see a strong young woman who has been through a lot of pain. They would see a young woman who didn't deserve what happened to her, or 'ask for it', but is healing and on the way to a better life! Most importantly, we can control how we see ourselves, recognize that we were victims and that we are now survivors.

The square world made me want to go back to what was familiar, my pimp and pullin tricks. I knew I was good at that at least, but going back was no longer an option because it would have been too dangerous. It wouldn't be until years down the line that I was able to begin deeply processing and able to be honest with myself about what had happened to me. I had been exploited. I was a victim of commercial sexual exploitation and domestic trafficking no doubt about that.

-Eliza

I was doing good and then something happened, and it made me want to go right back to the life. Am I ever going to stop feeling like this?

Yes, you will. We promise!! It's normal to have those moments when our feelings and memories get kicked up, or we get triggered. This can happen suddenly or gradually, and at any time or place. It can come as a shock if we felt like we were doing okay, and it can make us doubt our own progress.

Some feelings and reasons why we may go back:

- We're lonely.
- The square life is hard.
- We think it's the only thing we're ever gonna be good at.
- We miss the attention.
- We miss him.
- We felt like our folks were our family, and that we belonged.
- Our future feels so uncertain.
- Our wife-in-law was our best friend, and now we don't have any friends.
- No one will ever understand us.

I was at the park sitting by a water fountain, and I started to think about my folks. I remember we used to take long walks in this park that had a small lake in the middle. For a long time I just sat there and I couldn't help but cry because it's not like he was all bad. We had some very special moments and right now it feels like its happening all over again - he held my hand, was staring at me in my eyes and told me how much he loved me. I been away from him for a while now, and honestly this makes no sense to me how, I can remember this day like it was yesterday...

                                      -Marisol

There are different types of triggers. Some are **momentary triggers, like sensations**. For example, the smell of a cologne, a song that reminds us of our ex folks, a flashback to a strong memory where it feels like the situation is actually happening again, or a dream that we wake up feeling disturbed from. These are often related to trauma, and while they can shake us up in the moment, we can generally get through them if we practice grounding techniques, talk to someone we trust or write down our feelings.

The other types of triggers have more to do with **specific situations, events or ongoing feelings**. For example, breaking up with a new partner, someone we love passing away, the summertime or holiday season, not having money, fighting with our family, having our past thrown in our face. These types of triggers are sometimes harder to spot until we're already deep into the feeling of wanting to go back. The trick is to catch these feelings early on before they develop into full blown thoughts, plans and actions.

I started to think about the relationship that I had with my foster mother when I lived with her. I would never forget the time she said ' hell would freeze over before she let's a hoe sit at her table for Christmas dinner'. I'd rather be alone before I go back to her house. I don't have much family, so I am usually by myself from Thanksgiving all the way up until Christmas anyway. It is so hard for me to deal with being by myself and I hate the holidays because it is this time that I feel the most lonely and depressed..

-Jessie

In drug and alcohol recovery, individuals are told to

H.A.L.T. – Stop

when you're feeling: Hungry, Angry, Lonely, Tired. These four triggers are all natural feelings and sensations, but can make us feel like giving up and going back to old things, no matter how much progress we've made. Sometimes getting a meal or a good night's sleep can make all the difference in how we feel. Sometimes we just need to wait on a decision. If you really, really want to call your ex, try to wait 24 hours (or 12 hours, or 1 hour if you feel like you just can't hold off). Before you do anything, reach out and call someone supportive. Waiting and processing how we feel can give us a whole new perspective.

It's important to remember that just because we have a feeling it doesn't mean that we have to act on that feeling. Nor does it mean that we haven't made any progress or that it's a 'sign' that we're supposed to go back. Feelings aren't actions.

Sometimes I feel like a car

In the beginning I was fresh brand spanking new.

New rims, new leather seats, the whole nine.

I am the prize in his eyes that he wanted to drive around and flaunt in.

Then as time went by, through the months, through the years; through his

reckless driving with no caution or care

I get into countless of accidents.

There are new dents in the car, many scratches, and the engine

don't sound right.

The car shuts down, the window is busted and I'm in desperate need of a

new paint job.

The damage looks beyond repair and he is already on to the next

best car in the lot without even a second glance back at me.

I park myself away from him because it has become obvious even to me that

I need to work on myself and I just can't keep going.

So I begin to work on myself, put back some of the pieces that

were missing,

Change the oil of my soul and slowly I am becoming a brand new car again.

I build myself up, strong, revving my engine loud because I am angry,

hurt and it is still hard for me to forget all the repairs I went through to

get to this point.

I hate him for what he did to me and

I needed to let it out.

I needed to give him a piece of what's been on my mind.

A year and a half I've been parked

It took only 6 hours for him to convince me to open my car door to

let him sit inside.

It only took 6 hours for him to remind me how good it felt when he was behind

the wheel.

It took 6 hours of reminiscing about how we use to tear up

the road together.

It was 6 hours and I was right back with him.

I was his car again, he was the driver, and just like that; we were back

On the freeway hitting 90.

My life was in his hands

Destination unknown

Reckless driving

And all I could do is hold my breath and wait

Until the car loses control

More Scratches

More Dents

Busted out windows

A car still in need of repairs

Destined.....

For another car collision

-Selina

I feel so messed up. I just went back to the life. It felt like it all happened quickly, and now I'm back in and don't feel like I can try again to leave.

Even though it can feel like it happened quickly, we've often been juggling the idea of going back in our minds for a while. We might have stopped going to our program as regularly, or stopped talking about our feelings, or we may be dealing with one of the situational triggers mentioned earlier.

That's often when we begin the 'playing with fire' behaviors:

1. Hanging out with ex-wife in laws or cousin-in-laws.
2. Going near the track or clubs you used to work at.
3. Looking at ads on backpage.
4. Calling your ex folks and hanging up or having 'casual' conversations to just 'see how he's doing'.

We may tell ourselves that we can just dip our toe in the water, that we can just stop by to say hi, that we're not going to go back, but there's no way for us to just stay on the edge. Eventually, the life, or him or both will pull us back in.

I was out of the life for a lot of years and doing really well - good job, apartment, etc. I never, ever thought about going back to the game. I bought a brand new car and it was in a really bad accident a few months after I bought it. The car was totaled! And my insurance check was still in my purse cos I'd forgotten to mail it. At the moment when my car was upside down in a ditch, and I realized that I would still owe my monthly car payments for the next five years, and I was in shock and crying - all of a sudden the thought crossed my mind that I could make the money for the car in a few months if I went back to the life and this time I wouldn't have a pimp. The thought stayed in my head for a couple of minutes, and then I realized what I'd actually have to do to get the money and that I never wanted to have to do that with strangers again. And I told myself not to even go there, and the thought went away as quickly as it came. I've honestly never thought about it again. And yeah, I did have to pay the car payment for five years out of my check for a car that I no longer had. And it killed me every month. But it didn't kill me even half as much as going back to the life would've done. I can't even imagine now how that would've ruined my whole life. And now I have a better car, and I pay my insurance online and on time!!

-Rayne

Over time those moments get less and less frequent, and the temptation to go back gets less and less strong. Just because we had the thought or feeling of going back doesn't mean that we're not healing or that things haven't changed in our lives. People who used to smoke cigarettes will say that even though it might have been 10 or 20 years since their last cigarette, sometimes they'll have a sudden, random craving. That doesn't mean that the last 20 years of not smoking have been a waste of time, that they're still a smoker, or that they should go buy a pack of cigarettes! It just means that our brains can store memories and sensations for a very long time. Just because the thought comes, doesn't mean we have to act on it. It's good to figure out what our triggers are, and have a plan for dealing with them. For example, if the holiday season or summertime can bring up really hard feelings, get a summer youth job so that you're busy and have a little spending money, make a plan to spend Thanksgiving and Christmas with supportive people, or limit the amount of time you spend with family members who might upset you. No matter how much stress we have, nothing is really worth going back to the game.

Even though my new life was just beginning and things were somewhat getting better, I couldn't fight the urge inside of me to go back to him because I didn't want everything I went through to be in vain. I had to find closure, and I had to prove to myself that things were going to eventually get better with him and we were going to be together. I needed that from him, and more importantly, I needed everything he told me to come true. Once I went back it only got worse between us because he felt I shouldn't have ever left in the first place and started to check me for every little thing I did or didn't do. I was tired of him putting his hands on me, tired of fighting, and tired of him telling me that I would always be shit with out him. I felt so

stupid for going back. It wasn't a day that went by that I didn't beat myself up about being back with him. I started to miss how I was before I came back to him and all the positive things I was doing for myself. I began to remember all the good things in my life that were slowly happening for me while I wasn't with him. Going to all my appointments, getting up early to go to my program, taking the ged test, my counselor hanging my ged diploma on her wall, the bank account I opened, the money from the stipend check I was saving, and the part-time Outreach position I was going to apply for in the spring were all the things that I was beginning to accomplish and look forward to. These were the things that made me feel good and these were all the things that I accomplished for me and without him. I remembered what my mentor said to me. She said that she believed in me and that regardless of what I could always call her when things got rough. She said that if I was ever to go back to him, I ~~could~~ could always come back to the program and the doors will always be open for me. It was then that I knew that this life was no longer for me and I left him again. I called my mentor and then went back to the program. It was like I picked up where I left off and no one judged me for going back to him. At that point for me going back had helped me see all the good that was in my life at the time. Even though I was searching for closure with him, I come to realize that just living a happy and healthier life without him was all the closure that I needed.

— Selina

PROBLEM!

I had so many thoughts about leaving, but couldn't find myself actually doing it. It took my first criminal arrest for me to finally walk out. My first night in the bookings was horrible. I felt alone and dirty, and I knew he wasn't going to help me. Even when I came out of the bookings, I said I was going to walk out, but I ended up running right back to him because that's where I fit in and that's where I felt loved. In the process of going back and forth to court was when I really realized what was going on. Every time I went to court all I could think about was losing my kids, and that gave me the strength I needed to finally say no, and walk out.

-Shanay

Leaving the life and then going back is something that many of us have done and many of us have done more than once. Obviously, we're not encouraging you to go back to the life at all, but we want you to know that what you are feeling emotionally is ok. Feelings aren't right or wrong, they just are. But there are also ways you can work through these feelings, and work toward staying out. In substance abuse recovery, individuals are told to avoid PEOPLE, PLACES, and THINGS that are triggers. We all know what those are for us, so planning ahead of time for the people, places and things we need to avoid can help us to not relapse.

There's so much more for us than being in the life, and things do get better in time. Leaving is very hard, and we have all struggled with the inside battle of wanting to leave and wanting to stay. But staying out has led us to the beginning of living a life that is so much better.

I acknowledge my past and I embrace it. I say that because I can't change my past. It is what it is. For me it was a lesson learned in life, and the way god intended it to go, it did. I look at being a survivor as a blessing because at least I was blessed to say I don't have the same mentality anymore. I've been put down and I've been told everything I wouldn't be. A lot of people who wrote me off couldn't survive one day in my shoes (and that's just a "normal" day). Being a survivor to me is knowing I can do this, someone's there for me and I am never alone. It's knowing I have a say so in my future and I ~~can~~ can have one. I am not only a CSEC survivor; I'm a survivor at life PERIOD.

- Mary

My best friend is still in the life, and I'm not anymore. We went through so much together as wife-in-laws, and I don't want her to feel like I'm better than her now. Its hard because I want to help her get out but she says she doesn't want to.

We can find ourselves torn between our old friends and our new life. There are no easy answers when it comes to navigating these friendships. They are real, but they're complicated by the life and the trauma we might have shared. No one wants to be in a place where you feel like you have to choose. What you can do is begin to create some balance and set some boundaries for yourself, so that your friendship won't affect you in a negative way or impact your healing process. It is important for you to be able to take a step back from someone or something that may be pulling you in the wrong direction. This is in no way saying that you cannot be friends or that you need to "cut her off" completely, but maybe right now, where she is, is a bit too much for you to handle on your own. You could encourage her to talk with a counselor for support, you can let her know that you will be there to listen, and you can reassure her as a friend that you support and love her. Sometimes taking a step back can be more helpful than diving right into something that is beyond your control. You can always be there for your friend when she needs you, but what that looks like right now may be different. Finding the balance between how we can best support and be a friend while taking care of yourself, is not easy, but it is possible.

NO ONE IS PERFECT
TRUE FRIENDS

Being around one of my cousin in laws, who I met while in the life and then starting to hang out with once I left the life, was really really hard, because even though I was trying to change, I still found myself doing all the things that I was doing while I was in the game with her. Staying out all night, not going home, smoking, drinking, and partying were some of the things that began leading me down the wrong path that I didn't even know I was going down. We were pulling each other in the wrong direction, and before I knew it, everything that I was beginning to change about myself, like getting up early to handle my business, enrolling in school, trying to find a job, didn't seem as important to me anymore. The friendship I had with my cousin in law was having a negative impact on both of us, and it almost took me to lose everything I worked so hard for, to begin to realize it. I knew that I had to begin to think about the friendships that I had and the people I surrounded myself with moving forward, so that I can not only get myself together, but begin to live a different life. It wasn't until we gave each other that space and time away from each other to work on ourselves that our friendship was able to grow in a positive way. Even now years later we are both doing great and our friendship is stronger than ever before. We can even look back and reflect on our mistakes, laugh, and talk about how far we have come.

-Selina

FRIENDSHIPS ARE HARD!!!

Having a friend in the life can hold you back to a certain point with your recovery. There are many times when I explain things to my friend about leaving the life, and that I understand it's hard when you think you really love someone. I find myself asking her questions, and to my surprise, they all are the same answers as to when I was in the life. The difficult part is for me to open her eyes to see the same thing that I see now, because I see that she is scared and knows that she doesn't have no where else to go. But, at the same time, I know that she wants out and wants to do better for herself. Having her as a friend sometimes hurt because I want her to understand that he don't really care about her, and at the same time, it hurts me when she tells me that he does all these wonderful things for her.

-Desiree

Sometimes I go and hang out with this girl I met at the program. We're both out of the life, but she took me over to her ex-folks house last week, and I felt really uncomfortable. Nothing happened, but she invited me to go hang out with her again, and I don't know what to do.

Sometimes it's hard to know how to navigate new friendships when we're out of the life. Your friend may not see anything harmful about hanging out with her ex folks, but obviously it's a situation that's dangerous, and could lead to problems for both of you. This doesn't mean that you shouldn't hang out with her as you enjoy her company, but sometimes we have to learn how to hang out with friends in new ways. Most of our friendships in the past have either involved the life, or getting high, or meeting guys. We're not used to going to the movies with our friends or going to the beach. Perhaps your friend doesn't know that you felt uncomfortable so you should have an honest conversation with her. Let her know that you feel unsafe hanging out with her ex-folks, that you care about her safety and well-being, and don't think its safe for her either. Tell her you want to spend time with her but in a different and more positive environment. Hopefully she'll be open to that. But, if she's not, it might be best to step back and set some boundaries. You don't have to stop being friends with her at the program, but you can't put yourself in danger just to be friends with someone. You deserve to have friends, and you deserve to have fun hanging out in a safe, healthy, positive way.

I often found myself choosing between loyalty to myself and loyalty to the ones who were my so called 'friends'. There was a time in my life where I had to choose between my own happiness and the many harmful things my friends wanted me to do.

-Olivia

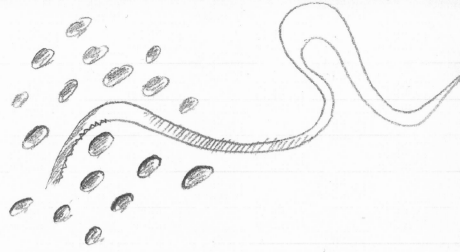

Am I ever going to make new friends? It feels weird being around a bunch of girls who've been in the life but we're not on the track anymore.

We all need someone who we can lean on for support. It is up to us to determine who we consider our friends, but that comes with time and really getting to know a person. Someone who is optimistic, encouraging, loving and who wants you to succeed, are just some of the qualities any friend should have. We have all found that being friends with other survivors is really important in our journey. Not every girl who has been in the life automatically has to be your friend, and you'll click more with some people than others, but our relationships with other survivors have been one of the biggest factors in our healing. We feel comfortable around each other, we don't judge each other because we've all been through the same thing, and we don't have to explain certain things like we would to people who haven't been in the life. Sometimes we sit and laugh about our experiences with each other, and sometimes we cry together. Both are healing and important. If you don't have any survivors in your community, build relationships online with other survivors. You'll be amazed at how much support and love is available.

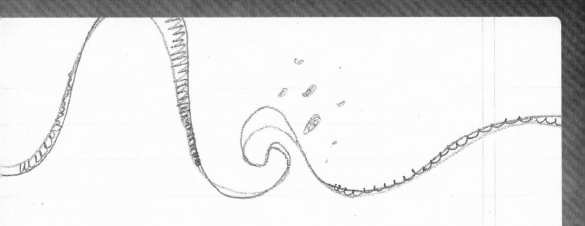

Now, being out the life and off the streets,
I realize how nice it is to have friends I can
talk to and chill with. I grew up in foster care,
and even though I had a twin brother, I always
felt alone. I had street family, but no one I
could really say wouldn't judge me or try to
get over on me. I was used to looking out for
myself and only for those who I felt were
going to look out for me. Being at my program
with other girls who have been through similar
things has helped me create bonds with people
I didn't think would be possible for me. I don't
have that best friend from elementary that I
still talk to or that roommate I had in college,
but I do have a bond with girls who I consider
my family, who have witnessed what I have, and
are staying strong for the future.

-Yvonne

Am I ever going to feel better?

YES!!!!! It's not like we can say 'after 6 months and 4 days, suddenly you'll feel better'. Healing and recovery come in little bits and pieces. Sometimes it feels like one step forward and ten steps back. But there will come a point when we look around and we're not crying all the time, we're not thinking about him every day, we're not walking around scared. We realize that we're healing, little by little. You've already taken the first huge step of leaving and beginning to get the support you need and deserve. There'll be bumps in the road, but you can make it through. One day you'll look back on this time and be amazed at how far you've come and how much better life is. There is truly life beyond the 'life'!

I really didn't know when I was growing up or when I was in the life that I could actually be this happy. Everything I saw around me was always pain and drama, and fighting and stress. I thought that I deserved all the bad shit that happened to me, and I didn't really like myself very much. Now I can honestly say that I love myself, and I love the life that I have. It's not always easy, but most of the time its pretty peaceful and happy, and I've got a lot of people who love me and support me. It took me a long time to fully get over my past, and once in a while something might remind me, but it doesn't mess with me the way it used to. I know who I am, and I know that I didn't deserve what was done to me. I'm proud of where I've come from, and I'm proud that I'm using what I went through to help other girls. It makes it feel like my life has a purpose. Now I don't regret what I've been through cos I wouldn't be where I'm at today if it wasn't for those experiences.

- Kimana

Continuing Your
Journey

-Survivor-

Who I was

A lost girl, lonely, who was manipulated and shamed
Mom gone and no one to care
Victim of home abuse
Emotionally, physically, and mentally broken down by the world
Which evolved around me

Who I am now

A beautiful woman who knows her worth
Stronger day by day
Becoming educated and motivated
Passing the knowledge onto the younger women
More understanding and aware
I am the definition, the constitution, and the breakdown of
A survivor

Who I will be

An educated woman
A future leader
A support system
A mother, a family person
A political figure
But of all
More than just a survivor
I will be an example, a statement, a dream
A hope

-Lakisha

-Fighter-

NO REGRETS!

Getting where you want to be is not the same as getting where
you need to be. Take your time and it will all come. Leave the
things you want behind, and go find the things you need.
Give yourself time to love yourself and heal from all the things
that have happened to you. It's ok to cry for the things that
were done to you and feel sorry for yourself, but don't let
that stop you from becoming a better you.

-Nicole

Love yourself, know you are worth more, and you have people that will and can support you. Never give up on yourself, and you are beautiful. A diamond that was in the ruff and you will blossom into a phenomenal, flawless woman.

—Ashley

For all the young women who are reading this, I want you to know that your past does not define who you are, that your goals are only within your reach. If you wanted to be a doctor at the age of 6, write down all the things that you need to do to become that doctor and follow it, and believe me when I tell you that before you know it, you will be in a hospital as a doctor. You have to learn and understand that everyone makes mistakes. It's what we do with our mistakes that make us who we are. —Desiree

-Faith-

It took a lot to see things from a different perspective, and be able to embrace my experiences and not regret them. I believe that if it wasn't for my experiences, I wouldn't be the person I am today. It is important to always believe in yourself, and know that you can be anything you want to be. It takes perseverance and hard work. As I continue to grow, I set goals for myself and make a plan for my life because I didn't want to keep going in circles and wanted a better life for my future.

I proved to myself that the impossible is always possible by being optimistic and making my dreams a reality. It is important not to dwell on the past, but remember that you can change the future. Everyone has problems, it's just how you deal with them. My past doesn't define me because I am so much more than what I was, and so are you!! I believe in you!!

- Ericka

Be
POSITIVE

Don't be afraid. I know that sounds lame, but this is a new beginning for you. I came from nothing and I learned to build, and now I can honestly say, I have something!! I don't have to answer to no one. I get to make my own rules and live my life like I always deserve to. You are strong, and you are here for a reason, regardless if you don't know what that is right this minute or what that can look like later on. Just know that you are special, loved, and it is time to put yourself first! I am here with you in spirit, and everyday I will continue to use my voice to make a difference for you, myself, and for girls everywhere who are so much more than our past!

−Cynthia

-Sisterhood-

For at least the first year after I left the life, I felt like I needed my pimp more than I needed air. I was in and out of shelters, I never had any money, all of my clothes were second hand, and I had the DA breathing down my back to testify against him. I was only 16, and all I knew how to do was get money. I'd dropped out of high school, I'd never had a job, and I didn't have any of my documents. I gave up on being a square every time I had to go through donations to find warm clothes that actually fit, every time I had to beg for an extension at the shelter, and especially every time I had to travel to a program just to eat. I was in a world where everything was new and boring. My views on love were so messed up. I mistook honest concern for mistrust. I hated the people that loved me the most. I didn't want help because I didn't realize how much I needed it. On top of that, many past experiences made me feel like everything had a cost - especially love and support. But one day I let my guard down, and I realized that the people at GEMS were more concerned about my safety and security than I was. Til this day, when I pass through my old stomping grounds, I remind myself that my past doesn't dictate my future. I cringe when I see motels that were built solely because of illegal demand. I pray when I pass tracks that are trading posts for innocence. And I do my best not to cry when I hear the most vulnerable youth in this city insist that they're immune to this issue. I can only hope that they hear what we're saying and hope that, if they find themselves in that situation, they remember that we exist. Sometimes it still catches me off guard that, even as a young adult, I'm showered with motherly love by people that have no blood relation to me. They want nothing in return, and have proven to me that they're invested in my well being for the long run. I'll always be a part of this family no matter what mistakes I make or where life's path takes me. Having such a consistently supportive network rooting for me makes that life seem dim and bleak. Having a better understanding of my experiences, and being able to relate to other survivors that are doing great things, has been priceless in my transition. I never realized that peer pressure could be positive. My peers constantly encourage me to further my education, find my place in the workforce, and find positive outlets to express myself. I'm having great time learning about myself, and I'm optimistic knowing that the best is yet to come! You deserve more than what you are going through or what you have been through, and I believe in you!   – Danielle

EXPRESS YOURSELF!

-Leader-

I know that you feel that where you are at right now is all that
it will ever be, but I am here to tell you that it isn't!! You
are strong, you are beautiful, and you are so much more than
what you have been through. It was hard for me to overcome
so many of the things that I had been through, to move past
all the hurt, and begin to believe in myself that I can have
a better life than the life that was given to me, but it made
me the person that I am. I no longer live my life in regret or
in shame of what has happened to me because I know that it
wasn't my fault, and I have NOTHING to be ashamed
of. I am a leader, role model, mentor, sister, friend, and a
good mother, and I have come a long way from my past. I
have accomplished so much and have so many things now to
be proud of, and I am living a life that I deserve which has

been longer than the time I spent in the game. Trust me, I know

it isn't easy because it wasn't easy at all for me and there were

many times I wanted to give up. The struggles I faced as a

young single parent and the many ups and downs I went through

was enough to knock me down to my lowest point, but I continued

to get up each and every time. I am grateful for all the people in

my life that saw the good in me, and loved me through the times

when I didn't love myself. Keep going and keep trying, even when

the odds feel like they are stacked against you, because you have

already survived, you will survive, and you are a survivor! I love

you, and I believe in you no matter what!

-Love always, Sheila

Life is Beautiful

-Growth-

When I was in the life I didn't always see myself. What I mean is, I felt my inner self becoming more invisible every day. In the beginning I felt so many different emotions in one day, and then few to none the next. The few that stuck through thick and thin were fear and loyalty. These are the two emotions that got me to survive. As much as I wanted to live, I had fear of him finding me and loyalty to my new family. My feelings had been so distorted I had no idea what I wanted, but I knew I was not going to get what I deserved by being in the life. Starting over and leaving was thinking too far ahead for me because sometimes I felt lucky to get to the next day. So when I finally left, I felt so vulnerable without any comfort, like my old clothes or a stuffed animal I really loved. I quickly realized that I'm now left with nothing. It was very difficult to just leave all my belongings and trust that these cops have my best interest at heart. Looking back now, I have pride in my actions. I never thought I would get my own place, my GED and start college. All these things took some time but they were happening, and I'm far from where I was when I got in the life. I have learned so much from what I have been through. Your past is what you have been through, but it does not make your future. Remember everyone has a past, and it's not where you come from, it's where you're going.

-Leslie

Although you are nearing the end of this guide, we want you to know that our love and support doesn't end here. You can join our online community that is specifically for survivors at **forum.gems-girls.org**, email us at **SLIinfo@gems-girls.org**, ask us more questions, or share with us your own journey and stories. Whether you connect with us, one of the resources listed in the back, another agency, faith-based organization, drop-in center, mentoring program or anywhere there is at least one caring, supportive individual, connect with SOME-ONE. While we are all strong and brave on our own, we all need support. Find your support person, then build a support network, and then grow it into a supportive community.

Read this guide as much as you can and as much as you want!! Pick it up when you are having a bad day or read a part of this guide every day in the morning to remind you of the future ahead. There is no specific order in the way we grow, or an exact way in which we heal from what has happened. Remember, you are strong, you are smart, you are beautiful, and you are precious. You are important in this world. You deserve so much more than the life. You weren't put on this earth to be bought and sold. There's a bright future ahead of you. It's going to take time and patience, and it'll hurt sometimes, but you're strong enough to get through it. You're a survivor! You made it through things that would have broken many people, and you're still here. We know you can make it!

We Love You and We Believe in You!!!
Your sisters at GEMS
xoxo

You are not your past   -Naomi

you deserve happiness!
love, Jessie ☺

It's time to put
yourself first
xoDanielle

love, Selina

YOU are not your past!
~Marisol

you're special! -Angie

You are a survivor!
besos, Mary
♡

love ya, Aileen

Keep going! love, Sheila

from your sister,
Cynthia

Survivors Guide
To Leaving

This is your time.
Love, Yesenia

We are here for you!
love, Eliza

WISHING YOU PEACE XX, DEE DEE

Keep your head up!
-Ericka

Don't give in to the negativity. xo Iris

You are brave
♡ Kristina

It's your life! ☺ Paris

big hug! Kimana

I support you!
⊛Pamela

Be Strong
love, Rhea

xoxo Jordan

If I can do it,
you can too.
love, Rayne

you have a whole
life in front of you.
☺ Janira

WE BELIEVE IN YOU
-DESIREE

YOU ARE STRONGER
THAN YOU REALIZE.
LOVE, CASANDRA

KEEP YA HEAD UP -SONDRAH

Stay hopeful!
♡ Lakisha

Love, Tamika

you are not alone. - Josalyn

P.S.

We strongly encourage you to connect with a program or organization. Here is a list of survivor led organizations and agencies that you can reach out to for support.

Girls Educational and Mentoring Services (GEMS)
New York, NY
(212)926-8089
www.gems-girls.org

My Life My Choice
Boston, MA
(617) 699-4998
www.fightingexploitation.org

Breaking Free
St. Paul, MN
(651) 645-6557
www.breakingfree.net

Veronica's Voice
Kansas City, MO
(816) 483-7101
Crisis Line: 816-728-0004
www.veronicasvoice.org

Courtney's House
Washington, DC
(202) 525-1426
Hotline (888) 261-3665
www.courtneyshouse.org

Bridget's Dream
Sacramento, CA
(916) 235- 3690
www.bridgetsdream.org

Treasures
Los Angeles, CA
(818) 986- LOVE (5683)
www.iamatreasure.com

Rahab's Hideaway
Columbus, OH
(614) 253-8969
www.rahabshideaway.org

Organization for Prostitution Survivors (OPS)
Seattle, WA
(206) 988-5463
www.seattleops.org

Dream Catchers
Chicago, IL
www.thedreamcatcherfoundation.org

There is H.O.P.E for Me
Orlando, FL
www.thereishopeforme.org

Survivors for Solutions
San Diego, CA
www.survivors4solutions.com

It is really important that you connect with someone so even if there isn't a survivor led organization in your area just yet; there are many programs and resources that you can contact to get the support that you need. The National Trafficking hotline number is free, available 24 hours a day, and they will assist you in finding a program in your state that best suits your needs. You can call any of these numbers at any time, any day, and someone will help you.

Polaris National Trafficking Hotline
1-888-373-7888
Text HELP to BEFREE (233733)

National Runaway and Homeless Hotline
1-800-786-2929

RAINN- Rape, Abuse, Incest, National Network
1-800-656-HOPE

Coalition to Abolish Slavery and Trafficking (CAST)
1-888-539-2373

Note to Self
If you have access to a computer and the internet; you can join any of these private online survivor support communities.

GEMS Survivor Leadership Forum
www.forum.gems-girls.org

National Survivor Network (NSN)
www.nationalsurvivornetwork.org

SHEILA WHITE

Sheila White serves as the Survivor Leadership Coordinator at Girls Educational and Mentoring Services (GEMS). She facilitates trainings on GEMS' innovative Victim, Survivor, Leader™ model for service providers, organizations, and CSEC serving agencies across the country. Sheila has been invited to speak in a variety of venues, including legislative briefings and conferences throughout the country, and more specifically at CNN and the United Nations. In 2012, Sheila was acknowledged by President Obama in a speech at the Clinton Global Initiative where recognition was given to both the international and domestic survivors of commercial sexual exploitation. Among many accomplishments, her advocacy efforts helped to pass the New York Safe Harbor for Exploited Youth Act. Sheila is a passionate and dynamic presenter, and stands as a strong advocate in the anti-trafficking movement. As a former member and graduate of GEMS' Alternative to Incarceration and Youth Leadership programs, she is a powerful role model, and inspiration to the girls and young women at GEMS.

RACHEL LLOYD

In 1998, at 23 years old, Rachel Lloyd founded Girls Educational and Mentoring Services (GEMS) with $30 and a borrowed computer. A survivor of commercial sexual exploitation herself, Rachel was driven by the lack of services for exploited and trafficked girls and the incredible stigma they faced. GEMS is now the largest service provider in the nation providing intensive services to over 350 girls and young women, preventive outreach to 1,500 youth and training over 1,300 professionals each year. Rachel is well-known for her tireless dedication to 'her girls' and has impacted thousands of individual lives, but she is also been passionate about changing public perception and policy. She co-produced the groundbreaking Showtime documentary Very Young Girls, seen by over 4 million people, and her courageous advocacy ensured the passage of NY's Safe Harbour Act, which in 2008 became the first law in the nation to protect rather than punish exploited youth. Rachel is also the author of the critically acclaimed Girls Like Us, and has spoken before Congress, at the UN and the White House.   In the last 16 years, Rachel has transformed the perception of trafficked girls from criminals to victims and now to survivors and leaders.

GEMS
Girls Educational & Mentoring Services

Girls Educational & Mentoring Services (GEMS) is the only organization in New York State specifically designed to serve girls and young
women who have experienced commercial sexual exploitation and
domestic trafficking. Girls Educational and Mentoring Services (GEMS)
was founded in 1998 by Rachel Lloyd in response to an overwhelming
need for services for girls and young women at risk for commercial
sexual exploitation and domestic trafficking who were being ignored
by traditional social service agencies. GEMS' programming is gender
responsive, trauma informed, developmentally grounded, strengths
based, social justice oriented, and culturally competent. GEMS' found-
ing principles reside in survivor leadership and transformational relationships. GEMS' services are based on the needs and interests of survivors and the agency's programming is developed based on survivors'
ideas, input, and expertise. GEMS provides young women with empa-
thetic, consistent support and viable opportunities for positive change.

$35.00
ISBN 978-1-4951-2932-2
53500>

9 781495 129322